Group of small musical boxes. *Top left*, composition snuffbox, decorated on lid with a miniature painted on glass. Contains a two-air movement, *c.* 1850; *top right*, amboyna-wood snuffbox with a similar miniature, containing a fine early two-air movement, *c.* 1820; *centre*, hand-painted tin box containing a two-air movement, *c.* 1860; *bottom*, tin box with transfer decoration containing a three-air movement signed 'Ducommun-Girod' on the comb, *c.* 1850

David Tallis

MUSIC BOXES:
A Guide for Collectors

STEIN AND DAY/*Publishers*/New York

First published in the United States of America by
Stein and Day/Publishers 1971

Copyright © 1971 David Tallis

Library of Congress Catalog Card No. 70–148834

Printed in Great Britain

Stein and Day/Publishers/7 East 48 Street, New York, N.Y. 10017
SBN: 8128-1371-5

Contents

Acknowledgments

It would not have been possible to write this book without making use of the knowledge and assistance of a number of people who have been most generous in giving their help.

In this respect I should like to give my thanks to Graham Webb for the loan of so many of his musical boxes; Dr Robert Burnett, President of The Musical Box Society of Great Britain, and Cyril de Vere Green, Hon. Secretary; Arthur Ord-Hume, Hon. Editor of the Society journal, *The Music Box*; Peter Ward, Ronald Pearsall, Robert Milne-Tyte and Gordon Savage.

The photographs are the result of many hours of tireless work by Peter Espe, and the items shown are from various collections: the carillon movement, the early movement facing page 33, the Serinette, the boxes by Ducommun-Girod and Grosclaude, the organo-piccolo box, the animated picture, the Seraphone and the German street pipe organ were all kindly loaned by Graham Webb. The Grande Format Forte Piano Overture box is from the collection of Dr R. Burnett; the three singing bird boxes and Viennese Musical clock belong to Mr C. de Vere Green; the musical watch and French musical clock, Dr S. Malitz (U.S.A.) collection; the Symphonion and Nicole drum and bell box, Dr B. Roughton; the Langdorf mandoline forte piano box, Grace Thompson; Grande Format Overture box facing page 81, Amos Fowler (U.S.A.) collection; the miniature barrel piano by Distin, Mr Austin Oliver; and the automaton dolls, Mr R. Sugden C.B.E. The automaton monkey is on display in the Wuppertaler Uhrenmuseum, Germany.

D.T.

Illustrations

7

Colour Illustrations

Introduction

We exist today in an age of noise from which it is extremely difficult to escape, and which has reached such a level that societies are formed to control it. Music is constantly in competition with other sounds, very different from its role of a hundred years ago. The music written then was not so brash as that of today and gave its audience pleasure by the use of more delicate subtleties of melody and arrangement. The audience actually *listened* to the music. So often now the music is written and played specifically not to be listened to; it's there only as a background to conversation, travel or, on occasion, the dentist's drill.

The musical box developed at a time when a big advance was being brought about in music. The size of public audiences was on the increase and their interest encouraged composers and performers to greater things. In 1787, Mozart produced *The Marriage of Figaro*, which was then an outrageous caricature of the social structure of the classes. It was written to be played before a cross section of the public rather than to the nobility, who had had almost exclusive rights to opera until then.

In the eighteenth century, the only way to bring music into the home was to play it yourself. Although many people could play a musical instrument, there were few who were skilled enough to keep up with the volume of popular music being written. There were no music-reproducing machines in the home except for chamber barrel organs, which seldom played more than hymns, dances or jigs. So in the nineteenth century music boxes began to be made in quantity, and they were designed to play all

9

the most popular operatic and orchestral melodies of the time.

Musical boxes were very popular and the demand for them became so great that it was extremely taxing on the skill of the makers. Extraordinary degrees of craftsmanship, which combined both musical and mechanical expertise, were attained in quite a short time. It is the combination of these two aspects, namely music and machinery, which is the chief reason for the interest shown by collectors today. People who are not mechanically minded tend to take the music for granted without realising how difficult it must have been for a watchmaker to put a musical arrangement onto a machine so that it could be played back as written.

Sometimes you can miss the appeal of music boxes by trying to consider them in a modern context. They were not made to be played in the 1960s. They were intended to bring the pop music of the nineteenth century into the drawing-room for the environment was of course entirely different from that of today. Even in towns and cities, life was quiet and people had much more time to listen. Since then we have invented many methods of transport whose noise interferes with our listening pleasure, and much of our time is also taken up with travel.

Into the nineteenth-century world the music box was introduced and eagerly accepted. The audience was critical but appreciative, and so the quality of music played improved rapidly, and the craftsmen achieving an amazingly high musical standard with such encouragement. The first music box to appear in anyone's house must have been a treasure indeed, surrounded with just a little magic, and it is this magic which the collector can recapture today if he approaches music boxes in the right way.

D.T.

1

History

Attempts were made to achieve some sort of mechanical musical reproduction in the third century B.C. when Plato had the idea for making a type of water clock which sounded the hours of the night on pipes, darkness making it impossible to read the face. Whether the clock was made is not known for sure, but it certainly marked a beginning in the effort to produce music automatically. A number of singing birds and organs which worked hydraulically probably were developed from this water clock.

With the invention of clockwork in about A.D. 1000 much greater advances were possible and it was not long before carillons of bells were made which played simple tunes pinned on a barrel. After this came the barrel organ, air for the organ coming from bellows driven by the clockwork.

A basic element of mechanical music is the storage of the music on the barrel or sheet, both of which can be considered the memory of the instrument. As with memory, the theory is that the data stored can be recalled at will, although the human memory is sometimes not as reliable as that of the machine. The music was set on the barrel in the form of pegs and pins and on the sheet as perforations or projections. When the barrel was rotated at a steady speed against a set of levers it was possible to make the levers play an organ or carillon.

The first mechanical instrument to appear in such a form was the barrel organ, the most famous of the early ones being the organ in Salzburg which Archbishop L. von Keutschach had made for him in 1502. It consists of 350 pipes on which music from a barrel is

played. There was only one tune for the instrument until Leopold Mozart composed eleven more in about 1753, and now only nine survive on the original barrel. The music is announced with a mighty cord, which among the locals has gained the organ the nickname of "the Salzburg Bull".

Carillons

Following the barrel organ came the carillon which provides a musical scale on a set of bells. At first they only played chimes automatically on the hour, but later, when the advantages of the barrel organ became apparent, barrels were pinned with melodies of great complexity, making it possible to play music which it would not have been practical to play by hand. The best carillons are to be heard in Flanders, as I am sure those who have travelled there will agree. A particularly fine example is to be heard in the square at Bruges. It was built into the cathedral tower in 1743 and plays really magnificent music. There are few greater pleasures than to enjoy Belgian cooking at a restaurant in the Markt while the world-famous carillon gives you a free concert. You can be sure that it will prove to be a very moving experience which you will find it hard to forget. Other fine carillons are to be heard in Antwerp, Ghent, Delft and Amsterdam. The Royal Dutch Palace in Amsterdam contains a carillon of 37 bells made in 1664.

Having made carillons in clocks and clocktowers, it was only natural that attempts were soon made to produce chiming watches. The first was made in 1686 by Daniel Quare who claims the honour for the invention. He made a watch which would strike the hours and quarters on a bell when the stem was pressed and released. The bell was fixed to the back of the case, and so the watch was by necessity quite thick. A watchmaker in Paris, Julien Le Roy, soon realised that it would be necessary to make repeating watches thinner, which he did by removing the bell and allowing the hammer to strike on the side of the case. Advancing from there, at some time during the second half of the eighteenth century he was responsible

for the invention of the spiral gong on which the hammers struck. The date is not known exactly, but Breguet made a watch with repeating work on gongs in 1785, so it can be reasonably assumed that the invention came some years before.

The Comb and Cylinder

By definition, the musical box is a mechanical instrument in which tuned steel tongues are set in vibration by means of pins set in a rotating cylinder or disc, and the invention was made as a result of all the developments already mentioned. The method of setting up music on a barrel was well known and had been used for many years on barrel organs and carillons, so it was only a short step from the gong in the repeater watch to the tuned steel tooth which could be plucked to play a note. The man to whom the invention is attributed is Antoine Favre, and the date of the invention was 1796. The authenticity for this date is taken from the records of the Society of Arts in Geneva for the 15th February, 1796, which reported that Monsieur Favre had found the means of producing a carillon without bells or hammers. Favre had, in fact, made mechanical music by fixing pins into the spring barrel of a clockwork mechanism and screwing a laminated stack of tuned teeth down so that their tips were played by the pins in the barrel. In this way the musical box as we know it came into being. It did not begin, as many would have it, as a pinned disc playing radial teeth arranged round it. The radial type of movement was a later development devised so that musical movements could be made thinner and be fitted into smaller articles such as watches and thin snuff boxes.

From Favre's stack of teeth and pinned spring barrel there developed the horizontal comb and cylinder at the same time as the radial movement. The first combs were sectionally made, each tooth being made separately and screwed down to the base of the comb individually, but as watchmakers became more skilled at the job they were able to make sections of two, three, four and five teeth until it was possible to make a complete comb all in one piece.

13

Beginning of an Industry

It took a little time for an industry to develop from the original invention of Favre. His idea was first used as an embellishment in snuff boxes, watches and seals, and no one thought of simply making a music box for its own sake. Philippe Meyland in conjunction with Isaac Piguet made some really fine musical snuff boxes with movements of the radial type at Geneva early in the nineteenth century; and then in about 1810 a group of watchmakers began to congregate there and organise the manufacture of small movements for watches and seals. Most of these newcomers to Geneva came from a watchmaking area in the Jura known as La Vallée de Joux, which was rather remote for a thriving organised industry. In this way the Geneva industry was started by Henri Capt, Les Frères Longchamps, Moise Aubert and Pierre Rochat.

Slightly later, in 1812 according to L. G. Jaccard, Jérémie Recordon made an attempt to start a similar manufacturing project in Ste Croix but it was not at first successful. In 1815 however, in company with Samuel Junod, he founded an industry at Ste Croix which made musical boxes of the larger type.

By 1815 in Geneva, the industry had become a source of prosperity for the manufacturers and a factory had come into existence directed by the brothers Henri and François Lecoultre. Another member of this family, David Lecoultre, was working in Ste Croix and it is said by Jaccard that he was the first maker to start making general use of the horizontal comb and cylinder type of movement instead of Favre's laminated stack of teeth or Meylan's disc.

After the industry had become settled, trade was brisk and the resulting development rapid. The musical boxes improved until by about 1870 they had reached their peak. By that time there was virtually no music which could not be played by them; it was possible to obtain variable volumes and tones on the same music box and it was also possible to manufacture a more or less unlimited number of barrels for the one comb.

The Cylinder Movement Mechanism

The cylinder music box movement is constructed upon a bedplate, usually made of brass, which is screwed into the wooden case by case screws and washers. On the bedplate are fixed the comb and cylinder and the clockwork to rotate the cylinder. On the left of the cylinder is mounted the spring barrel assembly which can be wound up either by means of a key or lever. It is kept wound by a ratchet. On the rim of the spring barrel is cut a wheel to drive the cylinder pinion, which is pushed onto the end of the cylinder spindle and kept in place with a taper pin pushed through the end of the spindle.

The right-hand end of the cylinder spindle has a large brass wheel, called the great wheel, fixed on it and the spindle itself is mounted at either end in brass bearings called the cylinder bridges. This great wheel meshes with a train of wheels and pinions which serve to let the spring run down at a constant rate. The wheel train consists of a wheel and pinion followed by a second wheel and its pinion. The second wheel meshes with the endless screw which is a vertical helical gear to which an air brake or fan is fixed. The endless screw and its fan regulate the speed of the movement and the more the blades of the fan are splayed out the slower the movement runs. A bearing or regulator bracket, often known as the cock, carries the endless screw. On top of the cock is a jewel endstone, usually made of garnet upon which the top pivot of the endless screw bears and rotates. The bottom of the endless screw is borne in a slide, which can be moved to alter the depth of mesh of the endless screw with the second wheel.

The endless screw is the part of the musical box mechanism which is by far the most prone to accident. If at any time it is removed or broken when the spring is wound, the entire force of the spring is discharged through without any resistance from the wheel train. The result is what is called a "run", and an enormous amount of damage can be done in a short time. As the cylinder spins round at high speed, cylinder pins are broken or flattened, and at the same time many of the teeth in the comb can be broken. The bass teeth

15

Early music box with the comb teeth screwed down individually; *c.* 1810

Carillon of bells playing music from a pinned cylinder. Fusee and chain driven; *c.* 1810

with its unlimited repertoire of music. It was mass produced and soon took over the market which had previously been the sole right of the cylinder box manufacturer.

The Phonograph

The success of the cylinder box lasted for about a hundred years, but that of the disc music box was really short-lived. The two major companies in Germany were in existence for about twenty-five years and the American Regina Company lasted a little longer, until 1919. A completely new conception of musical reproduction had come to pass. Oddly enough it resulted from an invention which was made before that of the disc music box. In 1877, Thomas Edison made his phonograph. He put on a record made of tin foil and recited into the horn the first line of "Mary had a little lamb", and with those words he made it necessary for you to collect musical boxes by searching for them in attics, instead of being able to buy one at the local shop.

It naturally took time for the phonograph to develop to a stage where it could effectively compete with the quality of cylinder and disc musical boxes, but by 1900 they had become more than just a curiosity. Wax cylinders were being made of the celebrities of the day and for the first time it was possible to reproduce an actual performance. It must have been a great thrill to hear Caruso at one of his recitals and afterwards be able to bring his voice to your home on a wax cylinder. Caruso was probably the first famous performer to allow his voice to be commercially recorded. That was in 1902, and it forced people to realise that the phonograph was not just an expensive toy.

2

Small Musical Movements

Small musical boxes are, perhaps surprisingly, in the same price range as the larger and more spectacular ones. However, since the musical movements are usually hidden from view in a snuffbox or similar item, you have a far better chance of finding a small box underpriced. This gives them great appeal to any adventurous amateur who wishes to build up an inexpensive collection.

Snuff and Snuffboxes
The habit of taking snuff developed when craftsmanship and extravagance were at their height. Respectable gentlemen who delighted in their own appearance, and who sought to please their ladies by speech and mannerism, created a ceremony of correct behaviour when taking snuff. This usually consisted of tapping the snuffbox three times to dislodge the snuff from the lid, taking a pinch between the forefinger and thumb of the right hand and placing it on the back of the left hand. It was then brought to the nose and "snuffed up with a sniff". The trappings associated with the taking of snuff were many, from the tiny mixing bowls and spoons for blending the snuff to the handkerchief on which you blew your nose.

The snuffbox, made in a great variety of forms and materials, was the ideal article on which the creative craftsman could show his skill. Snuffboxes have been made from practically every material, from naturally occurring seashells mounted with gold and silver to gold and silver themselves set with precious or semi-precious stones. At present, though, we must restrict ourselves to those materials used for musical snuffboxes.

Inevitably, as soon as watchmakers started to make small musical movements they had to find somewhere to put them, and snuffboxes were an obvious choice. They are an admirable choice for the collector. You could, if you chose, spend all your efforts in building up a collection of musical snuffboxes alone, and have a collection so varied that it would challenge any consisting of larger boxes.

Starting a Collection

A collection of musical snuffboxes can be started with three things in mind; you can look for beauty and value, or for boxes whose prime merit is that they play well, or boxes of historical interest due to their design or maker. It is not necessary, however, to restrict yourself to any one of these. A collection of beautiful and rare boxes which do not play well will never give complete satisfaction to their owner. Occasionally you will find a box which fits all three categories. You will be fortunate, and should be prepared to pay a considerable sum for your good fortune.

One such opportunity came to me a few years ago. I saw a silver snuffbox in a shop window and from its design could tell that it was an early radial movement of the type described in the previous chapter. The clue to this type of movement is that the box is smaller than usual, and normally has a single control button in front. At the time my car radio was playing *Variations on a theme of Mozart* and when I asked the shopkeeper to open the box it played the glockenspiel song from *The Magic Flute*—the same air I had been listening to. I found it impossible to ignore the omen and bought the box. As can be seen from the illustration (p. 48) it's of fine quality, a real collector's item. The hallmark was Birmingham, 1817, and the maker, Samuel Pemberton, a silversmith of some repute. Instead of having a winding square, on which the key fits, it is wound with a male key fitting into a square hole, a fact which confirms the presence of a radial movement. The music is started by sliding the control button to one side.

19

Materials

In the early nineteenth century musical snuffboxes were mostly made of expensive materials. If they were made of metal, then gold or silver would be chosen. A musical snuffbox of brass has been seen, but it is much rarer than one made of gold or silver. As manufacture progressed, however, it was found that the music sounded better in materials other than metal, and as the quality of the music improved and the tone became deeper, silver and gold were used less frequently.

Apart from precious metals, snuffboxes were made from wood, horn, tortoiseshell and composition. Those of wood are most attractive and often beautifully made. Usually a burr wood, such as burr-oak, burr-walnut and amboyna, was chosen, since the random direction of the grain made it possible to fashion the hinge without the danger of splitting. If you are lucky enough to own a wooden snuffbox you should inspect the hinge and then try it imagine the fine work involved in making a piece of such quality. The box illustrated (*frontispiece*) is made of amboyna wood, and the lid is fitted with a very fine *verre-fixée* miniature. Amboyna wood is full of tiny knots and burrs, the spaces between showing strong, dark lines. It originates from Amboyna Cay, one of a group of islands situated in the South China Sea.

Horn and tortoiseshell were really the first materials which can be compared with our present-day plastics. Both can be shaped at steam heat, and tortoiseshell, when heated rather above the temperature of steam and pressed against itself, can actually be welded together. Hence tortoiseshell boxes can be made without the aid of any additional adhesive. Incidentally, it doesn't come from the garden tortoise, but is obtained from the back of the Hawksbill turtle, which is divided into thirteen separate dorsal plates joined by ligaments into one complete shell. The plates are separated and the excess ligament scraped off prior to use. Like horn, tortoiseshell can be sawn, filed, polished and burnished to give the fine finish seen on boxes made of it. All musical snuffboxes have a tray inside for the

snuff. On the better-class early boxes this is sometimes quite transparent, made of a piece of clear yellowish tortoiseshell. On the later boxes cloudy horn was mostly used.

One of the first artificial plastics to be devised was a composition of ground horn and carbon black, which was pressed together under the right amount of heat. This material could be treated to a certain extent like a modern plastic and compressed into moulds. Articles made of it were cheap, due to their ease of manufacture, but their standard of finish was not as good as that of tortoiseshell.

Decoration

The lid of the musical snuffbox was the part mostly used for decoration. The plainest horn or tortoiseshell boxes usually had a small copper, silver or gold plaque set in the centre of the lid. Because tortoiseshell and horn become plastic when heated, it is possible to press pictures and patterns into the lids of boxes made of them. During the second half of the nineteenth century a large number of composition boxes featured views of Paris and other places. They were rather smart souvenirs and would have cost a pound or two, dependent on their quality, and most of them played adequately; if you're lucky you might find quite brilliant music in one of these cheaper cases. Earlier composition boxes were of better quality and tended towards scenes from mythology or battles rather than views of Paris. These boxes can be recognised by their superior finish and rounded edges and corners. They also have more expensive fittings such as gold or mother-of-pearl control buttons and a silver-gilt hinge. The snuff tray would be made of clear tortoiseshell instead of the later and inferior horn.

The lids of many musical snuffboxes were decorated with a miniature painted on ivory. Such paintings are usually of fine quality and a highly prized collector's item. A good artist to look for is Charles-Claude Delaye, who worked in France in the first half of the nineteenth century. One of his miniatures on a musical snuffbox is fitted with a gilt copper frame, and a bevelled glass. A slightly more

21

common form of decoration is the *verre-fixée* painting. This was a method of working where the picture was painted onto the back of the glass, the artist having to work back to front. It was then fixed with a layer of clear varnish and sometimes a sheet of gold leaf for protection. A development of this was to paint the picture onto silk first and then to stick the painting to the back of the glass with a clear adhesive.

If you are lucky you will find a musical snuffbox whose lid has been decorated with an Italian miniature mosaic. They are most skilfully made and not too common. If you are even luckier, you will find a box with a Swiss enamel miniature on the lid. The Swiss attained the highest degree of skill in enamelling, followed closely by the French, and then others from Battersea, Bilston and Vienna. If you doubt the claim that the Swiss were the best, look at an example under a magnifying glass. The work is quite beautiful, and the use of colour and soft shading exceptional. Such enamels are mostly found on the more expensive gold and silver boxes, but are also seen on those accessible to the more modest collector.

The variation in decoration of musical snuffboxes is limitless. A few were made of composition inlaid with silver in the form of bands and locks to produce an imitation of a cabin trunk in miniature. Others were inlaid with metals of different colours such as copper, silver, gold, brass and pewter to form an attractive floral design. It was even possible to construct a miniature 3-D picture made entirely of silver. Such boxes are not at all common and the decoration is called a *découpage*. Gold is also used for *découpage*. As you can see there is a great variety of snuffboxes to collect and it is therefore advisable to wait, rather than buy a box of doubtful quality or originality.

The Musical Movement

It was probably true to say that the outer case was seldom made by the watchmaker who was responsible for the musical movement. To buy a musical snuffbox the gentleman of the 1820s had several

alternatives. He could either go to the casemaker and select one ready made, or he could pay a visit to the watchmaker, from whom he could select the musical programme. The watchmaker probably had one or two movements in stock, and these would be displayed in plain tin boxes with pull-off lids, often painted dull grey. The tin box would give a degree of resonance for the music and would also serve to protect the movement during transit or storage. Occasionally movements can be found in their original grey tin boxes, the quality of which often belies the first class workmanship inside. If the purchaser could not afford to have the movement made up into an expensive snuffbox, he could buy it in a rather better quality tin case, fitted with a hinged lid and not a pull-off one as on the grey tins. The box would be decorated with a finely drawn transfer on the lid, and there would be transferred designs round the sides of the box.

The radial type of movement was an early form, but it is hard to believe that the music box began in this way, as is thought by some to be the case. Carillons and barrel-organs, which were much earlier in their conception, work on the principle that a row of levers attached to the notes is played by a drum, on which the tune has been laid out with pegs. This is not unlike the comb and cylinder musical box, so it is not at all unreasonable to suppose that the radial disc movement was a later idea designed to make movements thin so that they could be fitted into small articles such as watches.

If you find a radial movement, however, it will be early and date between 1800 and 1820. Some musical watches made after 1820 contain radial movements but it would be unusual to find a musical snuffbox of this type made later. The comb and cylinder were easier to construct and played much better.

Dating the Box

It is possible to date a small movement by careful study of its design. Strict rules cannot of course be made, but if features of design indicate a period which is confirmed by the type of box and choice of

musical programme, a fairly accurate guess can be made as to the date of manufacture. Already it has been said that the radial movement was made between 1800 and 1820; other dates are as follows:

Laminated comb: 1796–1810
Sectional comb in groups of 1: 1796–1820
,,   ,,   ,,   ,,   ,, 2: 1810–1820
,,   ,,   ,,   ,,   ,, 3: 1815–1840
,,   ,,   ,,   ,,   ,, 4: 1820–1850
,,   ,,   ,,   ,,   ,, 5: 1820–1850
One-piece comb: 1820 onwards.

Various other features can be used to assist dating. For instance, if the cylinder is hollow and without wax, giving the box a rather metallic tone, it is almost certainly earlier than 1820. Early combs did not have dampers, and so if a movement has an undampered comb, either the dampers have fallen off or the movement is prior to about 1825. Combs before 1830 were often made integral with their resonators. Later the resonators were made of lead and attached separately. Early movements were often made on a base plate of quite thin brass about $\frac{1}{8}$ in. thick. The normal gauge is $\frac{3}{16}$–$\frac{1}{4}$ in. and anything thinner could denote an early date of manufacture. If there is a bearing for the cylinder spindle separate from the spring barrel and close to it, the movement is early. This arrangement was displaced after 1830 and the shaft borne in a hole directly in the spring barrel. The top of the spring barrel is flat on early boxes and domed after about 1840, and the Geneva stop on early movements was of a different design. The angle of the cock over the endless screw also gives a clue to age; on earlier movements it tended to be placed parallel to the edge but later on it was screwed down at the corner of the base plate and came in at an angle. Let it be clear that there are very many exceptions to the above points, but if all features are taken into consideration it should be possible to date the movement to within about five years.

There is only one way to be completely certain about the year of

manufacture. If the box is silver or gold and English, it will have a hallmark which can be looked up in an invaluable book called *Guide to the Marks of Origin of British and Irish Silver Plate*, by Frederick Bradbury. This booklet shows all the hallmarks of the major assay offices from the mid-sixteenth century to the present day. Another useful book is *Silver Collecting for Amateurs*, by James Henderson. Continental marks are complicated and you usually have to be content with a bracket of ten to fifteen years. They can mainly be found in three books: *Hallmarks on Gold and Silver Plate*, by W. Chaffers, or *Les Poinçons de Garanties Internationaux pour L'Argent* and *Les Poinçons de Garanties Internationaux pour L'Or*, both by Tardy. French silver marks are not commonly known and it is worth remembering those which often occur on musical snuffboxes. The hare's head is seen on very many silver hinges on the better class tortoiseshell or horn boxes, and the fasces mark is the Paris mark of

guarantee for 1809–19. Both these marks are very small and are best read with the aid of a magnifying glass. Reading hallmarks is not easy if they are worn, and takes some practice. Most people use an eyeglass and strong direct light. It is far easier to see the contours of the mark if an oblique light is used, and sometimes the outline of a worn mark will show more clearly if you breathe on the metal. Incidentally, if you do breathe on a silver article your breath condenses on it in proportion to the purity of the silver, so cracks and repairs will show up quite sharply.

The Musical Programme

The programme of music varies from two simple airs to an abridged operatic overture. The majority of early boxes play two

airs and by sliding the right-hand control button to the left or the right, you can select either tune. Radial movements occasionally play two tunes and this is done in one of two ways. Either both sides of the disc are played at once and the tune changes ever half revolution, or one tune is pinned on each side of the disc, which can be moved up or down between two sets of teeth so that one side only plays at a time. The latter are less common and can have two control buttons on the front of the box, which gives the appearance of a cylinder movement. Later cylinder movements were made with a snail-type of tune change and these could be arranged to play two, three, four, five and even six airs. I have a box which plays twelve airs on a $2\frac{3}{4}$ in. long cylinder. There are six positions of the cylinder and two airs are played during the course of each revolution. When bought it was in a really terrible state and will require about five years' work before it plays. It is interesting to know, however, that such movements were made and to have a record of the fact.

Perhaps the finest music played on small music boxes was operatic. A stop mechanism was designed by which the cylinder came to rest only after every other revolution, and it was thus possible to spread the available playing time over two revolutions. Using this method quite ambitious programmes could be set up, and the operatic aria was ideal. The first revolution could be used for the slow recitative and the second for the quicker finale. An ideal aria for this would be *Una voce poco fa* from *The Barber of Seville* by Rossini, and I myself have a box which plays the final duet and finale from the second act of *The Thieving Magpie*, also by Rossini. This is on a box made by Henri Capt in about 1840, and it plays superbly. One of the very best and most sought-after makers, Henri Capt seldom made a bad box. Another air often heard on an aria-type movement is *Bid me discourse* by Bishop, who wrote the music of *Home, Sweet Home*. I own one by Nicole Frères which plays this air, and there is another box where the same air has been set up by M. Bordier with a slightly different musical arrangement but no less pleasingly.

26

The Makers

Certain makers regularly made good quality movements of the small snuffbox type. M. Bordier, who worked in Geneva in 1815–30, made movements which nearly always played well. Henri Capt is one of the best of all, and never seemed shy of the complexity of the music. The arrangement on some of his movements was often so involved that the spring had to be made stronger in order to drive the cylinder round against the resistance of so many teeth being played at the same time. Nicole Frères made many small movements which were always of good quality, and if you are lucky you will find one signed by them. Various members of the Lecoultre family made snuffbox movements, but they are not often to be found. A small movement by H. Rochat is not common, and a prize indeed for the collector. He was too busy making singing birds to spend much of his time on music boxes. The initials PM in a diamond denotes Piguet et Meylan, a firm of repute. They worked between 1811 and 1829, making particularly good radial movements. A fine small movement maker was François Alibert, who worked in Paris between 1820 and 1850. I have seen many movements with his name stamped on the baseplate or comb, and others with his signature scratched on the baseplate, spring barrel or cock. It is possible that these were not made by him, but just passed through his hands for adjustment or repair. Alibert's musical movements are often seen in the hollow wooden bases of French clocks.

Sewing Boxes

A very attractive item for the collector is the musical sewing box or *necessaire*. Some of these are really quite early and contain most interesting movements, which are screwed down to the bottom of the wooden sewing box. A tray in the top carries the various items of sewing equipment, some of which are nearly always missing and hard to replace. Magpie thimble collectors are quite relentless when they spot a gold-mounted mother-of-pearl thimble in a *necessaire* and it is often the absence of the thimble which spoils the set. The

27

box itself can be in many forms, such as a miniature grand piano veneered with walnut, maple or mahogany, and decorated with boxwood stringing. A casket shape is also common, such boxes usually being veneered with a burr-wood and sometimes mounted with a pierced silver or steel decoration. The underside of the lid is fitted with an early mercury-silvered mirror.

The sewing box illustrated (*facing page 33*) is quite plain, but it contains a very interesting early movement with its sectional comb in groups of two teeth. It has the early type of Geneva stop, and there is a separate bearing for the cylinder spindle at the spring barrel end. The cylinder itself is without wax and the baseplate is only $\frac{1}{8}$ in. thick. All of these features point to the pre-1820 period, which is confirmed by the silver mark on the top of the cut-glass bottle. It bears the Paris mark for 1809–19, so a fair estimate for the date of the box would be 1815.

Manivelles

Young children have many times been the cause of the ruin of a music box. There was however, a design which was simple and robust so that a child could use it and cause a minimum of damage. Such movements were called *manivelles* and it is said that they originated in Vienna in about 1840. The comb and cylinder arrangement was set in a stout wooden box or a round tin, and to the great wheel on the end of the cylinder was geared a worm drive which could be turned with a handle. In early *manivelles* the music was often operatic and well set up, but as time went on it was realised that the child could not appreciate the difference between a well-set-up cylinder and a poor one and so the standard of music inevitably fell. Later *manivelles* often had two or three different tunes which were so shortened that they were barely recognisable. Rarities to look for in this field have bells, which play very sweetly. A *manivelles* with a drum is also known: it is quite early and plays well but you would be very lucky to find another. Early *manivelles* are often in quite plain mahogany cases, with nothing to show that they are

musical except for the handle which projects through the top of the case. Later the top was often decorated with a picture of a child or a group of children.

Poupées

A rather unusual form of *manivelles* is the *poupée*, or musical doll on a stick, and it is consequently quite rare and expensive. It looks just like a jester, similar to the doll carried by a medieval court fool. Most *poupées* were made from about 1860 onwards and contain a *manivelles* type of movement, the stick being attached to the worm drive so that as the doll is waved round, it revolves and the music plays. They often played operatic airs which have been quite well set up. It is rare to find a *poupée* which is still dressed well, for as they were continually being spun round the silk fabric soon became tattered. If you have to repair one try to use only real silk of an age and texture similar to the original.

Family Albums

The musical family photograph album is worth having in your collection. There are quite a lot about and it is worth waiting for a good one to turn up. These large photograph albums are in two parts; the first half for the pages of photographs and the second a container for the musical movement. They are leather-bound and often quite handsomely tooled and gilded. Like all old leather-bound books the back is the weak spot and many are to be found with split spines. The musical movements nearly always seem to have been made by the firm J. G. M. et Cie., and no one seems to be sure what these initials stand for. The music is of good quality however, considering that many of the movements were made in this century. If you buy a musical album, try to find one with the photographs still in it. Photography was still fairly primitive and the ceremony associated with taking a picture will be amusingly evident in your album. While in the hands of its original owner the album was probably brought out on display when relatives and neighbours

came to tea on Sunday. There was no television to distract them from the photographs and life was quiet enough to allow them to hear the music undisturbed.

If, as a new collector, you cannot decide what kind of music box to collect but wish to specialise in one particular aspect, you could do no better than choose small movements and snuffboxes. A collection of fairground organs is a difficult thing to shelter, but a large number of snuffboxes can be kept in a drawer. Also, if you wish to take part of your collection to a friend's house you can put it in your pocket, more congenial than arriving with an organ in a removal van.

3

Large Musical Boxes

The quality of the music which can be played by a small movement is somewhat limited by the size of the comb and cylinder and so it was the large music box which attracted most makers. We have already seen that the first movements were used merely to embellish a small article such as a snuffbox; the music was not of great merit to begin with and only the simplest of melodies could be played. After a while, however, the watchmakers became more ambitious in their musical programme. They started to make movements for the sake of the music alone and all their efforts were concentrated on improving its quality and complexity.

Early Improvements

The date of birth of the large music box according to John Clark was about 1820, although you may be lucky enough to find a few experimental models which were constructed before this. Usually those before 1820 were made for clocks and would be fitted into the oval wooden bases on which they stood. The earliest of these clock movements can be quickly recognised by the design of their comb and motor mechanism. The combs made before 1810 were sectional with teeth arranged in groups of one or two and the spring barrel was often connected to the cylinder with a fusee and chain. The fusee is designed to give a constant source of power to the mechanism as the spring runs down, but this is not an essential design for the music box.

31

Improvements to the Cylinders

The first cylinders were drilled, and the pins then forced into the holes so that they fitted tightly and firmly. In about 1810 it was found that a thin layer of wax run into the cylinder would ensure that the pins all stayed in place. An early cylinder box without wax is recognized by its metallic tone.

The method by which the music was set on the cylinder is always a point of interest for visitors to your collection. The procedure was as follows:

(a) The cylinder would be turned from brass and then set on its spindle.

(b) The cylinder on its spindle would then be put onto an apparatus which pricked the pattern of the tune on the cylinder. This pricking machine was capable of controlling accurately the rotation of the cylinder to give the tempo of the music. The punch to mark the music was attached to the end of an arm, which could be moved in accurate intervals along the length of the cylinder. To mark a note, its position in the music would be noted and the cylinder revolved until it corresponded. The punch would then be moved along until it was in register with the note required and a mark would be made on the cylinder.

(c) After the cylinder had been marked with all its music, it was sent away, usually to people who worked at their homes, where it was drilled ready to take the pins.

(d) After drilling, the pins were inserted. This was a most laborious task, since some of the cylinders had as many as 10,000 holes in which pins had to be inserted. This operation was also completed by outworkers and they used sticks of wire, which had been nicked at $\frac{1}{4}$ in. intervals so that the end could be inserted and snapped off quickly. After a time special cutters were used, and for these the wire had to be softer; it is usually a sign of an early box for it to have pins of very hard and brittle wire.

Viennese Grande Sonnerie clock with musical move-
ment playing on the hour; *c.* 1815 (Presented to Mr.
C. de Vere Green by The Musical Box Society of
Great Britain on the occasion of his retirement as
Hon. Secretary of the Society)

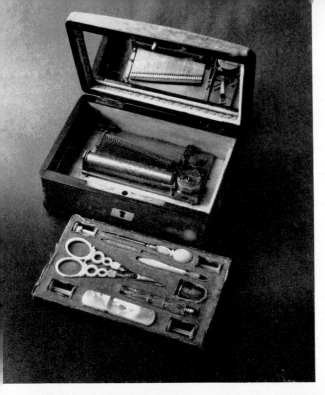

Georgian necessaire containing fine early musical movement with comb teeth screwed down in pairs, *c.* 1815; *below,* early movement with sectional comb in groups of four and a typical plain fruitwood box to house it; *c.* 1820

(e) After the pins had been inserted the cylinder was warmed and a quantity of special cement would be melted and poured in. The cement is similar to sealing wax and consists of a mixture of shellac, pitch and brick dust. This is firm when it is solid, but also has the desired characteristics when molten. After the cement had been poured into the cylinder, heat was applied, and the cylinder rotated rapidly, so that the molten cement was thrown to the wall of the cylinder, flowing round the pins. When the cement was completely liquid and just coming out of the holes in the end plates of the cylinder, the heat was removed and the cylinder spun until the cement was absolutely hard.

(f) The cylinder was then shaved by turning it in against a lathe cutter until all the pins were the same height. The pins were finally given a slight upward tilt to make them impinge on the comb teeth at the correct angle.

(g) The final stage was to test the cylinder on the music box, and this was done by the man who had carried out the original pricking. He would play all the tunes through and make minor adjustments by bending the pins, and a few mistakes would have to be broken off. It was during this finishing process that all the skills of the watchmaker became evident.

Development of the One-piece Comb

It is said that the first comb constructed from a single piece of steel was made in 1815, but one-piece combs certainly were not in general use until about 1820. It is unusual to find many music boxes made at this time which are signed with the maker's name, but occasionally I have seen very early movements with one-piece combs which were signed by H. Lecoultre, Lecoultre et Falconnet, Falconnet et Reymond, R. Nicole or Françs Nicole. It seems that the one-piece comb was first in regular use in Geneva where Henri Lecoultre and his brother François had their factory. They may well have been the first to exploit the invention.

c

Nicole Frères

More music boxes of a consistently good quality were made by Nicole Frères than any other maker. They made very few poor music boxes, so that when a collector finds one bearing their name he will usually find that it plays well if in good condition.

Until 1970 it was accepted that Nicole Frères were the two brothers François and Raymond Nicole, who worked independently during the first half of the nineteenth century before joining forces in 1839 to form the company Nicole Frères. In the 1969 Christmas edition of *The Music Box, Journal of the Musical Box Society of Great Britain* an article challenged the previous theory and gave a great amount of supporting evidence, demonstrating that previous historians may have been wrong. The article resulted from the original researches of Mr C. de Vere Green and Mr A. W. J. G. Ord-Hume, both founder members of the Musical Box Society, and the latter the author of *Collecting Musical Boxes and How to Repair Them.* Following an exploratory visit to Geneva, Mr de Vere Green learned from the State Archivist in that city that although there was a François Nicole in Geneva making very fine boxes during the first half of the nineteenth century, he had no connection with the firm Nicole Frères, nor was he related to that family. His third child however, a daughter, did marry a Henri François Raymond, which could have led to previous François and Raymond Nicole theory.

The new concept of the history of François Nicole is backed by the existence of very fine overture boxes which can be found to bear the signatures "Franç.^{s} Nicole" or "Raymond-Nicole" on the comb. These boxes appear to have come from the same workshop regardless of the name with which they have been signed. They are of the very highest quality and were made around 1820. The cylinders are about 10½ in. long and 2¾ in. in circumference and are usually marked not only with the register lines but also with lateral lines so that the entire cylinder is divided into tiny squares. Their combs have about two hundred teeth and are works of art in themselves. Three tunes are usually played, sometimes three overtures but often

two overtures are followed by two arias from the operas in question, both of the latter being played during the course of the third revolution. These fine movements are usually found in well-made but plain cases, so it is possible to walk into a shop and out again without even noticing such an ordinary-looking box!

Those who admire early Nicole overture boxes will appreciate an anecdote from New Jersey, U.S.A. There are two collectors, good friends with a common interest in musical boxes. The first has a large and very fine representative collection of cylinder and disc boxes of the larger type, which occupies most of his cellar space. An item in his collection is an overture box signed "Françs Nicole" with the serial number 3. It is a most interesting box not only because of its extreme rarity but also because it plays impeccably. The second collector has a fine collection consisting mainly of the snuff box type of musical box.

It happened that the local saleroom had a music box for sale which was similar to the François Nicole, except that it had been signed Raymond-Nicole. It was viewed by the snuff box collector but because he had to go away on business he asked his wife to bid for him. She was sitting in the saleroom waiting for the lot to come up, and then who should come in but the other collector. Rather than do battle over the box it was decided that he should buy it and then discuss final ownership when his friend returned from his business appointment. He bought the box.

That evening the two rivals sat either side of a small table. On it was the Raymond-Nicole musical box, a bottle of whisky and two glasses. The arguments were simple: the man who had seen the box first did not possess a similar item and he felt that not only should he claim ownership but also that it would fit into his collection much better than that of the other. The man who had actually bid for and bought the box already had one by François Nicole, so he felt that it was not only legally his but that it was fair it should come into his collection. By 4.0 a.m. they had talked continuously for six hours, finished the whisky and decided nothing.

There was only one solution, and the coin they spun still lives in the music box, which is now in the collection of the gentleman who did not have one before. Luckily they live close enough to one another for the unlucky loser to play the box from time to time.

The Formation of Nicole Frères

According to the Geneva Archivist, who has provided the evidence for the researches of Mr de Vere Green and Mr Ord-Hume, the firm of Nicole Frères was the result of a partnership between the brothers David Elie Nicole and Pierre Moise Nicole which was established, according to the company's letterheads, in 1815. Since there was no commercial register in Geneva until 1883 the date cannot be finally confirmed, but it is known from other records there that Pierre Moise, having spent some time away from Geneva, returned in 1812, and in 1815 went to live at his brother David Elie's address—rue des Étuves 223.

The company established, the two brothers started to produce musical boxes of the highest quality. Every box was stamped on the bedplate in the left hand corner "Nicole Frères à Genève", and the combs were stamped "Nicole Frères". Sometimes even the individual components of the wheel train are stamped NF. All Nicole Frères boxes are numbered and it is possible to make a close approximation of the date of their boxes from the number. Nicole Frères, of course, had their own tune sheets which were of fairly simple design but always had the maker's name and the number of the box written on them. Also written on Nicole tune sheets is the "gamme No."; this is the maker's index number for the tuning scale of the comb.

Music Played on Early Boxes

The very first music boxes played the simplest and best known of melodies. As they were not played so well it was essential that the music was recognised, so you will find that the very early boxes play traditional airs and dances which were already well known to

everybody. Soon however, as the quality of the movements improved, it was possible to make them play new tunes and so the operatic repertoire was the obvious favourite. The music of Mozart was the first to be used regularly and overtures or arias from *The Magic Flute*, *Don Giovanni* or *The Marriage of Figaro* occur often on the early boxes. I have a box dating from about 1810 with teeth screwed down singly which plays an air and three variations from *The Magic Flute*, oddly enough the same air as that played by the silver snuff-box mentioned in the previous chapter. Rossini wrote and produced *The Barber of Seville* in 1816, and in 1821 Weber's *Der Freischutz* had its opening night in Berlin. Both operas were full of arias ideally suited to the musical box and the overture to *Der Freischutz* has probably been transcribed on to more cylinders than any other overture.

The Overture Box

Although the early nineteenth-century operas were full of good melodies to be played by music boxes it was the operatic overture which presented the greatest challenge to the makers. An overture is usually full of orchestral light and shade and it was the representation of this which attracted them. Even in the earliest overture boxes they attempted to pin the individual parts of each instrument and this was done with remarkable success. You can even pick out many of the instrumental parts by putting a short roll of tissue paper on one particular section of the comb. The only shortcoming was that it was not possible to play a sustained note and this is represented with a trill. Popular overtures of the time were Rossini's *William Tell* and *The Italian Girl in Algiers*; Bellini's *Norma* and *La Sonnambula*; Auber's *Fra Diavolo* and Weber's *Oberon* in addition to those already mentioned. Such was the popularity of Rossini after the production of *Tancredi* in Venice in 1813 that he was nicknamed "the barrel organ composer". As ambitions became greater, overture boxes were made bigger and with thicker cylinders in order to give the longer playing time required, and these boxes have become most sought after by all collectors.

Boxes with Two Tunes per Turn

Given a thick cylinder, it does not mean to say that it must be set with a single piece of music for its complete revolution. Many boxes were made to play two or occasionally three airs for one turn of the cylinder. The more teeth available for the music, the better the quality will be, and so the best way to increase the number of the tunes played is to divide the cylinder's revolution. This is far preferable to setting up a greater number of tunes with a full turn for each. If this is done the teeth have to be more widely spaced and their number is thereby reduced. Many twelve-air boxes with two tunes per turn were made but you may find a few of the earlier variety with eight tunes arranged in this way.

The Forte-piano Musical Box

Soon it was felt that there was virtually no complexity of music which could not be played by a musical mechanism, and further improvements to their performance were made. The first of these allowed both soft and loud music to be played by means of two separate combs. Nicole Frères made the first forte-piano boxes in about 1840, and because of their popularity with collectors they are hard to come by. They really play beautiful music. They can well represent an operatic aria as an accompanied solo, but sometimes a forte-piano box will play an overture and this really is a treasured prize. The loud section and its bass accompaniment is played on the longer of the two combs while the shorter comb is made to play parts of the melody with less volume.

Improvements to the Case and Controls

For the first twenty-five years musical box cases were made of fruitwood without decoration of any kind. Cherry, pear, rosewood and elm were often used, and only the simplest butt joints were used. Occasionally this austerity was carried to an extreme and the lid would be attached with brass rings instead of hinges; very rarely was there a lock, the lid being secured with a hook and eye arrangement.

The control levers on these early boxes project through the end of the case on the left-hand side, and the winding square for the key also shows through the end. There are three control levers; the one to the rear being the change lever, which determines whether or not the tune is repeated or changed; the centre lever is the stop-start lever, which starts the mechanism and then permits it to stop at the end of a tune; finally, the lever to the front is the instant stop, used when the pins or dampers are to be adjusted. It is unwise to stop a mechanism for long periods in the middle of a tune, since the pins and teeth which are in the middle of playing a note at the time would be strained and bent by the pressure on them.

It is most unusual to find a box decorated with inlay work with the control levers through the end. The first major change in the outward appearance of the box was that an end flap to the case was designed to cover the control levers when the box was not in use. This end flap was generally used after about 1830. At the same time as this development the cases began to be made with a compartment at the right-hand end in which the key could be kept. This was a most sensible idea since a loose key in the box could cause damage when the box was moved or carried. It is a good tip to collectors to remember to keep the key either in its compartment or on the winding square. Also, when you take the key from its compartment to wind the box, it should not be carried over the comb. If it is dropped, a broken tooth will almost certainly be the result.

By about 1830 it had been found that if more attention was paid to the case and its design, a better sound would result. The use of a broadgrained softwood for the base of the case proved to be a most effective sounding board for the movement and gave far greater resonance. The movement was made with feet under the bedplate so that good contact was obtained between the movement and the bottom of the case. Also the sides of the case were fitted with a wooden shoulder, which was tailor-made to fit the sides of the bedplate. It was inevitable that this attention to the case led to its greater decoration, which took the form of exotic veneers over the

39

entire surface and simple banding round the edge of the lid. Very soon, however, the decoration became more elaborate and marquetry designs were applied on the lid. Rosewood was the veneer most used and the design would be inlaid in satinwood or boxwood. On the more expensive cases the use of mother-of-pearl, ivory, silver, pewter and enamel can often be seen. The case decoration naturally put up the price of the box and economies soon became necessary on the cheaper musical boxes. After about 1850 only the best were veneered all over and the run-of-the-mill case would only have a decorated lid.

Mandolin Music Boxes

The mandolin is strung with four pairs of strings, each pair tuned to the same notes as the four strings of a violin. It is played with a plectrum to produce melodies with a tremolo effect. Composers have not often written music specifically for the mandolin but it has been used on many occasions to produce a dramatic effect with its romantic sound and associations. That old reprobate, Don Giovanni, having convinced Donna Elvira that he loves her, arranges for her to run off with his disguised manservant, whom she mistakes for Don Giovanni himself. As soon as they have gone, he takes the centre of the stage and proceeds to serenade her maid with a mandolin.

The music of a mandolin music box, like the instrument itself, paints pictures in the imaginative mind, and such boxes are very popular with collectors. Luckily a great number were made and they are therefore not difficult to find, but you may have to pay a little bit more than you would for a music box of the normal type. The secret of the mandolin effect is in the comb. Groups of teeth are all tuned to the same note, and these are plucked by the pins on the cylinder which are arranged to play a trill. It is necessary to have many teeth for one note when a trill has to be played because it is not possible to pluck the same tooth twice in quick succession. Time must be given for its vibrations to die. The majority of mandolin

Grande-format forte-piano overture box by Nicole Frères No. 36790. The lid is decorated with rosewood veneer, inlaid with brass, tortoiseshell, mother-of-pearl and enamel, c. 1860

The stamp "G" on the comb might well stand for Giuseppe Verdi, but so far the maker has not been identified. One thing is certain, the box was made during or very soon after 1853.

Other composers were well represented. Meyerbeer, whose music is much underestimated now, had written *Les Huguenots, Robert le Diable* and *Le Prophête,* and music from all three appears on many boxes. The *Ra-Ta-Plan* song from Donizetti's *La Fille du Regiment* was very popular and you will find it on many boxes, mandolin and otherwise. The overture from Auber's *Crown Diamonds* is often heard and dates from 1841. In 1847 the composer, Flotow, wrote an opera called *Martha.* It is not often heard these days but you will understand its success at the time when I tell you that the main aria in it was *The Last Rose of Summer.* The tune became so well known that most people forget that it was part of an opera.

The air which was used more than any other on musical boxes was first heard at Covent Garden in May of 1823. In his opera called *Clari, the Maid of Milan,* Henry Rowley Bishop, an Oxford University professor, introduced the public to *Home Sweet Home.* The tunc was used repetitively during the opera and it made such an effect on the audience that it is still alive after 147 years. Not only is *Home Sweet Home* a good tune, it is one which can be remembered; also, it sounds so well on a musical box that it might well have been written especially for that instrument. Nicole Frères made a few so-called "Extra Grand Musical Boxes" which played variations on, amongst other melodies, *The Last Rose of Summer* and *Home Sweet Home,* the variations on the last being those which had been written by Thalberg. The music is very complex, and tested the skills of the musical box maker to their utmost. These variation boxes look like overture boxes with a thick cylinder and finely cut comb but when you hear the music made by them it really sounds like the ultimate in mechanical music. Perhaps a point of perfection had been reached beyond which no progress could be made.

Rare Types of Early Music Boxes

Before about 1860 manufacturers had found it possible to market musical boxes without having to mass-produce them. The individual attention given to them allowed the music to be reproduced to a very high standard although the different types of music box being made were limited. The forte-piano box was the first experiment and when these boxes appeared the forte-piano effect was produced on a single comb. It was the cylinder which produced the loud and soft contrast by having long and short pins. Such boxes are quite rare and should be valued as such if you find one. They were usually made by the Lecoultre family and I have seen single-comb forte-piano boxes by both David and François Lecoultre.

A few forte-piano boxes were also made with mandolin combs and these are pleasant to the ear. The difficulty in making forte-piano mandolin boxes arose from the problem of making the soft comb audible over the resonance of loud trills of the larger comb. Nicole Frères made one or two and I have also seen forte-piano mandolin boxes by Ducommun Girod and Langdorf. Some very fine overture boxes were made with long and soft combs and occasionally a Nicole Frères forte-piano mandolin overture box can be found.

Mid-nineteenth-century Changes to the Mechanism

It was in about 1860 the lever wind came in. The key was easy to lose and it could damage the comb if dropped, so the lever wind was a natural result. Also, and slightly earlier, makers started to construct the case with an inner glass lid. A sheet of glass supported with strips of wood was used at first, and then the glass lid was hinged so that it would protect the movement when the outer lid was open.

Sublime Harmony

Occasionally, as you listen to a forte-piano music box, you'll hear it produce a particularly striking resonance; it occurs when the two combs are playing the same music in unison and is a very

pleasing effect. In 1874 Charles Paillard made a box with two combs of the same length tuned to the same scale which could play the music in unison. This Sublime Harmony arrangement, as it came to be known, was a great success and he patented the idea the following year—U.S. Patent No. 161,055. The best way to describe the resonant effect produced by these boxes is to compare them with a stereo record player plus twin loudspeakers; the music is brought into the air instead of staying at one focal point. It was not long after invention that sublime harmony boxes were made with three or even four combs all playing at once. Sometimes one of the combs would be a mandolin comb and these very melodic boxes were called "Harpe Harmonique" music boxes.

Nineteenth-century "Folk"

The folk music of the second half of the nineteenth century consisted almost entirely of an interminable number of Scottish airs, if music boxes are anything to go by. My northern cousins will probably think me a terrible Sassenach, but some of these melodies really are very dreary. Many eight-air Scottish boxes sometimes sound as though they are repeating the same tune over and over again. Great numbers of boxes playing Scottish airs were made, so if you get one make sure it is a good one. I once saw a specimen which played very indifferently, so the proud owner had embellished it with a tartan cloth which was stuck to and covered the lid.

Far more collectable are hymn boxes. Perhaps because of their sacred nature, more trouble seems to have been taken over the arrangement of the music. The first boxes to be made with sacred airs came in about 1830, and they were produced regularly after that date, although never in large numbers. Most hymn melodies are simple and consist of a number of large chords played at regular intervals. This type of music sounds particularly well on a music box but it must have been most difficult to produce. The pins had to be set with great accuracy for all the teeth of a twelve-note chord to be played at exactly the same time. The *Elijah* of Mendelssohn and

Handel's *Messiah* were popular at the time and their music was frequently used; *Oh, rest in the Lord* from the former is very often found on hymn boxes. The longer sacred airs were transcribed on to music boxes with thick, overture-type cylinders, but such items are rare.

Later Types of Overture Box

Overture boxes remained very popular items and so they were made at prices to suit all tastes. To give you some idea of the original price of musical boxes, the following are taken from the 1888 catalogue of Wales and McCulloch of Ludgate Hill, agents for many makers including Nicole Frères.

Six Airs	£4	4	0
Six Airs, Mandolin	£8	0	0
Six Airs, Sublime Harmony	£8	5	0
Six Airs, Mandolin Forte-piano	£12	10	0
Twelve Airs, Forte-piano	£10	0	0
Extra Grand Music Boxes			
Four Sacred Airs, Forte-piano	£20	0	0
Four Variations	£23	0	0
Four Overtures	£20	0	0

It must be realised that these prices represent a lot of money at that time, but they have had a smaller price increase than many other antiques on the market today. You can draw a comparison, of doubtful value, with another contemporary advertisement taken from the *Illustrated Times* of 1856:

UNSOPHISTICATED GIN—The strongest allowed by law, of the true juniper flavour, and precisely as it runs from the still, without the addition of sugar or any ingredient whatever. *Imperial gallon*, 13*s*. Henry Brett & Co., Old Furnival's Distillery, Holborn.

The final item mentioned in the musical box catalogue is the "Grande Format Overture Box", and it could be supplied with forte-piano accompaniment for another £4. These music boxes are amazing if only for their proportions. The cylinder is about two feet long and four and a half inches thick, the comb having about two hundred and fifty teeth. It is obvious that if you are going to make something of that size that it should only be of the finest quality in every way. I have never heard a bad Grande Format Overture Box; if it plays badly it is probably because either the teeth are worn or the pins are bent, but it is unlikely that one of poor quality was allowed to leave the factory. Because of the length of the comb the extent of the music which could be played is more or less limitless, and because of the size of the cylinder many overtures could be played in their entirety. You will also find that every care was lavished upon the cases of these boxes. Expense was less of an object than with the smaller variety so all types of decoration and inlay was used. Brass, silver, mother-of-pearl, tortoiseshell and enamel are all to be seen.

The cylinder of a Grande Format Overture Box probably has up to 50,000 pins. If you find one which requires repinning it is always worth having it done, if the comb is in good condition. It may be three or four years before you get the cylinder back and it will be costly, but if you call yourself a collector then you should feel it your duty to see that these fine pieces are restored whenever possible. About three years ago I had the opportunity to buy an early key-wind Grande Format Overture Box. The comb was only missing one or two teeth but one of the overtures had been stripped completely from the cylinder as the result of a run. I was asked £50, which was a lot of money then for a damaged box, but I know now that I should have bought it. The cylinder would now be due back from Switzerland with a bill for about £75, but the value of the box would exceed by far everything spent on it.

Interchangeable Cylinder Boxes

One of the disadvantages of the music box was that each box was limited to the music transcribed onto its cylinder. If you wanted more music, you had to buy another music box. In 1850, however, it became possible to make a musical box which had more than one cylinder to fit it. So it was now possible to buy your music box complete with a set of three or four cylinders which could be interchanged. This was fairly simple to achieve with a system of levers on the cylinder bridges which locked or released the cylinders. Later, in 1875, Amédée Paillard improved on the invention and brought out a patent—U.S. Patent No. 212,108—for the production of cylinders which could be interchanged on any machine of a particular series.

Because musical boxes were now being supplied with a large number of extra cylinders, it became necessary to pay more attention to the piece of furniture which housed it all. It is not possible to make a case which is capable of taking the movement and more than three or four cylinders, but many interchangeable machines were made which were supplied with up to ten cylinders, so a table with drawers had to be supplied. Usually the table model music box is itself a pleasing piece of furniture, and is sometimes also designed for use as a writing desk.

Piccolo Music Boxes

In a flute band, the piccolo player is selected because he is in command of the instrument and also because he has an inventive musical mind. During the course of a march and usually in the quieter third section or trio he takes the piccolo and plays a solo part which rides on top of the rest of the music with trills and scales. It is a shrill instrument playing an octave above the orchestral flute and giving the highest notes to be obtained by the orchestra. It was only natural that the music box maker was soon making a comb which could play the piccolo part. At first a separate comb was used which looks like a continuation of the main comb but it was soon easy enough to make the whole comb in one piece.

Piccolo boxes are strident to the ear as a rule but if the high-pitched section is used to accompany a sublime harmony arrangement, a very pleasant sound will result. If you see a sublime harmony movement with one comb longer than the other, like as not it will be a sublime harmony piccolo box. A good number of the boxes were made, but they are often of large proportions and of the interchangeable type.

Drum and Bell Accompaniment

This is the first of the "gimmicks". I do not use the term disparagingly, but when the comb and cylinder was not enough, other means of producing sound had to be introduced. Even the makers were not too sure of themselves when the first drum and bell boxes were made; they hid the bells and drum away under the cylinder so that they could not be seen. The drum was made of brass or tin and nothing would have been gained by showing the source of the rather distasteful noise. The bells were attached under the bedplate in a stack and they were struck with hammers attached directly to the underside of the comb teeth. If the hammers are adjusted properly the bells play quite sweetly and sound well as an accompaniment to the comb.

Later, all was exposed and tune sheets bearing the words "Drum and Bells in View" appeared. The drum at this stage was made presentable, and at the same time more pleasant to the ear. Instead of being made completely of metal, it was constructed like a real drum with a proper drumskin made of parchment. The bells were arranged on a gantry behind the cylinder and often engraved or silver-plated. The hammers to play the bells were attached to the comb with a system of levers and were sometimes decorated to look like bees or butterflies. Unfortunately, all these decorative embellishments allowed a sale to be made even if the music was below standard. Very often I have heard a rapturous description of the little drum and the butterflies from someone who remembers nothing of the quality of the sound. If you are considering buying a

Above, fine silver snuffbox by Samuel Pemberton of Birmingham containing a Swiss radial type musical movement, 1817; *below*, two fine quality musical snuffboxes with miniatures painted on ivory on the lids. The movements are exposed to show a one-piece and a sectional comb in groups of three. The box on the left, *c.* 1840, is signed 'Delaye' and the right-hand movement, made about 1815, is signed 'H.C.'

Miniature English Barrel Organ or 'Serinette'. *c.* 1830

Fine three-overture box by Nicole Frères, No. 21550, in a fruitwood case, *c.* 1840

bell box, look for one with at least six properly tuned bells. I really think it is to your advantage to do without the drum. Drums and bells were first used on music boxes in about 1860, and they became visible about ten or fifteen years later. A further source of noise to drown the comb was the castanet or wood block. This is a fairly common embellishment to a box but fortunately it can nearly always be switched off at will by the listener.

Zither Accompaniment

The other gimmick often seen is the zither attachment. It is a roll of tissue paper which can be lowered on to the length of the comb giving it a deadened plucking tone. It was intended to imitate a zither but in my opinion does not achieve much of value. The tissue paper is held in a hinged arm so that it can be lowered on to the comb at will, but it is often the source of many unwanted rattles and vibrations. It can also hold moisture and cause damage due to rust which will be very detrimental. Originality can well be dispensed with by the removal of the zither altogether.

Back to the Barrel Organ

It is surprising that it took so long for the musical box makers to combine the comb and cylinder with the barrel organ. As we have already said the barrel organ is an instrument which dates back to the fifteenth century and since the musical box developed from it, it was an easy step to put pegs and bridges on the musical box cylinder so that an organ could be played. A reed organ was used and it usually had between ten and twenty notes. It is unnecessary to say that such boxes are ideally suited as hymn boxes. At first brass accordion-type reeds were used singly, but later it was found that if the reeds were used in pairs, a more vibrant sound was produced. Such boxes were stated on the tune sheets to have *"Voix Celeste"*—heavenly voices—accompaniment. Good organ boxes are hard to find for your collection. If you find one in need of repair, it will result in extra work due to the complications involving the organ mechanism, so buy warily.

The Orchestra Music Box

Finally we have the music box which has everything. The full orchestra box, which is usually an interchangeable machine with bells, drums, castanet and organ. Sometimes you even find dancing dolls inside the case, jogging up and down in time to the music. These boxes are large and command high prices, but somehow the magic has gone; the music of the comb and cylinder is now lost in the clatter of the drum and castanet. You are paying for more machinery but get less music for your money.

Types of Extreme Rarity

There are a few types of musical box which are so rare that if you find one, it may be one of as few as a dozen survivors.

The Duplex Musical Box was made in 1887 by Alfred Junod at Ste Croix. Two cylinders were played at the same time by two combs. Such boxes are extremely rare, but there is one in the collection of Mrs Ruth Bornand in New York, which is illustrated in Graham Webb's book *The Cylinder Musical-Box Handbook*. Another can be seen at the Pitt Rivers Museum, Oxford.

A rare type of mandolin box is the Organoclied Music Box. The mandolin comb is normally arranged so that the trills are only played by the treble end of the comb, while the bass plays a simple accompaniment. On an Organoclied box the bass also is given a mandolin-type arrangement of repeated notes, and this builds up a very powerful dominant chord which resonates in a similar fashion to an organ pedal or persistent bass note. Organoclied boxes are unusual and worth keeping a look-out for.

I know of only one music box with an organ played from the cylinder and no comb. It plays well but is really only of interest due to its rarity. Although built like an extended organ box it is not a musical box in the true sense of the word. It is in the collection of Mr Cyril de Vere Green, founder member of the Musical Box Society of Great Britain.

Perhaps the most impressive piece of machinery in the musical box

field is the Revolver Music Box. Invented by Amédée Paillard at Ste Croix in 1870, it consisted of a set of cylinders fixed on a rotating shaft so that any one could be brought into contact with the comb at a time. In this way the repertoire of a box could be greatly increased. There are three illustrations of revolver boxes in Graham Webb's book, one being a fine mandolin box by Nicole Frères. It has six cylinders, each playing six airs; a repertoire of 36 airs without table or drawers. However, they were so difficult to make that very few are to be found.

It was the wish of a few makers that your music should be accompanied by the song of a bird and so the comb was combined with a small set of flute pipes which played to imitate birdsong. The bird was represented by a small automaton either on top of or in the front of the case. The early *Pièces à Oiseau* are of good quality and play quite well, but later nothing was gained by the bird other than the novelty of the idea. They are extremely rare in spite of this and an example would make a valuable addition to your collection.

Complete overtures usually could not be played because of their length and they had to be abridged, but a way round this was found in the Plerodienique Music Box, which was designed so that it did not have to stop the music while the cylinder was being moved. This is achieved in a most ingenious way. Two combs are played by a cylinder which is constructed in two halves, joined with a sliding joint at the centre. When the music on one end stops so that it can move along, the other end continues playing so that there is no perceptible break in the music.

Finally we come to the Polytype Music Box. I know only of one of these machines, made by Paillard, Vaucher, Fils. It is an ordinary-looking box and plays six airs on two combs, but the musical arrangement is adjusted so that two airs are played sublime harmony, two are played forte-piano and the last two are played harpe harmonique. Three sounds for the price of one!

4

Disc Musical Boxes

The first major revolution in the history of music boxes came almost a hundred years after their invention. And revolution it was, for it involved the introduction of the revolving disc to play the comb instead of the cylinder as had previously been the case. Cylinder boxes were expensive to buy and limited in their repertoire, twelve tunes per cylinder being the most which could be played without loss of quality. The interchangeable table model was bulky and expensive and so makers started to think of ways which could extend the repertoire of a single machine. The idea of the disc set with music in the form of projections stamped on it was born in the mind of Miguel Boom, who lived in Port au Prince, Haiti. He patented a large music box in which a steel disc or music sheet revolved under a comb, causing it to play the music set on the disc. U.S. Patent No. 267,482 was taken out in 1882, but it was not commercialised since the design made it hard to change one disc for another, thus showing no advantage over a cylinder box.

In 1886, Paul Lochmann of Germany designed a music box on the disc principle by causing the comb assembly to revolve beneath the disc or tune sheet, as it is sometimes called. His patent—U.S. Patent No. 346,757—came from the idea of an Englishman, Ellis Parr, who was the first to appreciate the importance of making a machine with readily interchangeable discs. The discs of the first Lochmann music box were made of card. Holes cut in the card caused little levers to operate and play the comb. The cards soon wore out and so they were replaced by steel discs, and the holes replaced by projections. These projections, stamped out of the

steel, played directly on to the comb, which was revolved under the disc by means of a clockwork motor.

The Symphonion

In 1889, one of Paul Lochmann's workmen, Paul Wendland, realised how unsatisfactory their methods of plucking the comb had been and invented and developed the star wheel, which was immediately patented by Lochmann. By this time the machine was called the Symphonion and rapidly became a great success commercially. All the popular tunes of the day could be set up on the discs and so the machine never became out of date like the cylinder box. The Symphonion was to be found in cafés and taverns, where it soon paid for itself if fitted with a penny-in-the-slot device. The mechanism was fairly robust and could withstand heavy use, and the discs were thrown away and replaced when damaged. Because of their durability and quality, Symphonions are often found today and can still be bought at quite reasonable prices. They are always named but can be recognised quite easily because the disc retaining arm extends right across the diameter of the disc.

The Polyphon

The late nineteenth century was a time for industry and competition, so it was not possible for Lochmann to reap all the benefits of his invention for long. Two enterprising young men who had learned how to build disc music boxes while employed by Lochmann were soon competing with him. Gustave Brackhausen and Paul Reissner started in a small way but soon had a large factory in Leipzig quite close to the Symphonion works. They employed a thousand people and produced great numbers of disc music boxes of all shapes and sizes. The inevitable happened: Lochmann challenged the Polyphon Company and took them to Court for infringement of his patents. Polyphon defended the case on the grounds that the projections used on Polyphon discs were completely different from those on Symphonion discs, and were their own invention. A Polyphon projection consists of a single strip of steel

stamped from the disc and bent right over so that it supports itself. If you compare it with the Symphonion projection you can see it is of two strips stamped from the steel, one to turn the star wheel and the other to support the first. Polyphon won the case and continued production with renewed strength. Lochmann appreciated the advantages of the simpler Polyphon projection and adopted their design himself. Both firms continued to work to full capacity for a market which at that time could not be flooded. The demand was enormous. In addition to the two great companies, many other smaller firms started and some of the cylinder box makers went over to disc music box production.

Drama was added to the Polyphon story when, in 1899, a great fire destroyed nearly the whole factory overnight, but although the building suffered considerably most of the machinery was undamaged. When the workers arrived the next day they set to with production of Polyphons in the temporary buildings which were soon erected. Very soon the factory was again working to full capacity and continued to do so until 1914.

The Regina Disc Musical Box

The manufacture of the disc machine was more a matter of production planning and machine design than manual craftsmanship as in the case of cylinder boxes. Comb tuning was still a difficult job though, and Swiss craftsmen were sought after for this work in Germany. Disc production was easy. Once the master disc had been set up, very little skill if any was needed to operate the machine which made copies of it. Setting up the music on the master disc required experience, and the man who did this work for Lochmann was a Swiss called Octave Chaillet, who came from Ste Croix where he had been employed in setting music on to cylinders. After a few years at Leipzig, Chaillet went to America to join the Regina Company at Rahway, New Jersey. The Regina Company had been started in 1892 by Brackhausen, whose Polyphons had been such a great success in the States that he decided to leave Leipzig

with a nucleus of craftsmen and start his own business there. The Regina music box started as a copy of the 15½ in. Polyphon and used the discs being made at Leipzig. After a short time, however, such was the success of the company that Brackhausen wished to be independent of Leipzig for the supply of discs. It was for this reason that Brackhausen asked Chaillet to join him in Rahway, so that he could start the composition and production of new discs. A number of negro spirituals and Souza marches were set up in addition to the tunes already available from the Polyphon factory.

The Regina developed a tone entirely different from that of the other musical boxes of the period. Even the Polyphon, upon whose design it was based, plays with a harsher tone than that of the Regina, which was able to play loudly and yet with an extremely mellow sound. The use of different steels radically alters the tone. The Regina Company went into the construction of the wooden case in greater detail than was done in Leipzig, and in addition to screwing down the ends of the bedplate of the movement also placed a sound post between the middle of the bedplate and the bottom of the case. This sound post, absent in the Polyphon, causes a far greater resonance. My own collection, which consists chiefly of cylinder boxes, has one disc music box and that is a 15½ in. Regina table model with two combs, which is by far the best disc machine for its size. The two combs are tuned almost identically, the difference being just enough to give a sublime harmony effect. The Regina achieved near perfection when it was decided to shorten the bedplate. Instead of being screwed down to either side of the case, one end was screwed directly onto the sound post in the centre. This design produced a tone which few music boxes have been able to equal. Short bedplate Reginas are rare and a prized item for your collection. The Regina Company continued until 1919 —much longer than the European firms, which had mainly closed down during the Great War. By that time, though, business must have been almost at a standstill because the music box had been completely replaced by the Phonograph.

Autochange Machines

It's all very well to have a music box with interchangeable tune sheets, but you'll soon find out as the owner of one, that, unless you are prepared to get up and change the tune every minute or so, then the same melody will repeat itself until the spring has wound down. A cylinder box does at least play all six or eight tunes of the cylinder in turn. Brackhausen realised this could be a possible disadvantage and invented the autochanging disc machine in 1897. Up to twelve discs, kept in a rack below the movement, are lifted up one at a time on to the centre spindle to be played. After being played, the disc is lowered back into the rack again. It is possible on such a machine to select discs at will with a selector lever, or to set the machine so that it plays all twelve in turn. There are two separate clockwork mechanisms, one of which plays the disc while the other raises or lowers the tune sheet. Early autochanging machines had two spring barrels but later on the makers were able to design the mechanism so that both motors could be driven from one spring. Autochange machines are quite large and although the Regina Company made them for 15½ in. discs very few come to light, and so far I have never seen a 15½ in. Autochange Polyphon. The most usual size is the 24 in. diameter Autochange Polyphon, but Regina made a very fine autochanger for 27 in. discs, called the Regina Orchestra Corona. They are not uncommon, but are in such great demand that they are very expensive. It is certain they play as well, if not better, than any other disc machine ever made.

Multi-disc Machines

The Symphonion Company made large disc machines which played two or three discs at the same time. Those which played two discs simultaneously were usually horizontal table models and are extremely rare. The normal single disc models played on two combs, but four combs were brought into play by the two discs, thus giving a sublime harmony effect. The discs are in pairs, number one and number two, and must be put on in the right order. The Eroica

three-disc model was also made and produces a beautiful sound. The discs are 14 in. in diameter and the whole machine stands 81 in. high. The Eroica works from two motors geared together and very fine piccolo and harmonic effects are produced by it.

Bells, Chimes and Organs

A fine Polyphon worth looking for is a small table model fitted with twelve bells. The $14\frac{1}{8}$ in. discs play the two combs to the accompaniment of bells and the sound is certainly very pleasing. Glockenspiel chimes were often substituted for the bells and it is not uncommon to find a Polyphon of this type. The chimes can be switched on or off at will by moving a lever. Many of the autochange Polyphons were fitted with chimes. A massive music box called the Polyphon Concerto was virtually an orchestrion, and this played piano strings, a glockenspiel, a snare drum and a cymbal all with a 32 in. disc! Perhaps the most ambitious of all though was the Fortuna 26 in. which played magnificent music on two 118-tooth combs and a small drum as well as a 14-note reed organ. A real orchestra indeed!

The Stella Disc Machine

Of course, it wasn't only Germany and America who capitalised on the new popularity of disc music boxes. It was Switzerland with all their years of experience with cylinder boxes who made the greatest variety of machines. Their production did not equal that of the Polyphon factory, but in quality there was little to choose. This was especially true of a disc box made by Mermod Frères called the Stella. It was the first of the Swiss disc boxes and was an improvement on the German machines in that it played discs which had no projections. The points of the star wheels show through a steel plate which covers the combs and they are turned by holes in the discs. This design does not make the box play better, but it does certainly protect the working parts. The comb teeth are completely covered by the steel plate which not only protects it from damage but

also stops bits of dirt from falling into the star wheels. Stella music boxes were brought to an extremely high finish, visible parts being chromium-plated, and you will usually find that this finish has lasted through the years. It's hard to believe they were made between 1895 and 1901.

The Britannia

A product of the Swiss firm of B. H. Abrahams, the best known Britannia is the Smoking Cabinet model. Standing about two feet high it is in the form of a small cupboard in which pipes and cigars can be kept. There is a transfer of Britannia on one of the doors which makes identification very easy, and the musical mechanism is inside the cabinet. A small disc with a diameter of only $9\frac{1}{8}$ in. plays the comb. A comparatively short comb makes a truly grand sound. Although its tone can be a little strident, the little Britannia produces an enormous volume of sound which comes from the back of the cabinet. This is made from broad-grained sheets of wood designed to resonate like the soundboard of a grand piano. Larger Britannias were made and had the same design of backboard with side panels which could be opened to give even greater resonance than before. The larger models of Britannia are fairly rare, but you should be able to pick up a small Smoking Cabinet quite easily.

The Kalliope

This is the box which winds up through the centre of the disc. They are not very common and since they do not possess any distinguishing features other than their method of wind, it is an opportunity for the collector to find a rare box at a reasonable price by using a little specialist knowledge. Few general dealers will appreciate the significance of the winding hole being in the centre of the disc. You will occasionally find a small Kalliope with eight bells, and most of this make were fitted with a zither attachment.

The Sirion

I mention this disc machine not because it is one which you are likely to find but because of the interesting mechanical development incorporated by it. This is the only case known where it was possible to play two tunes with two revolutions of the disc. In a way, it tried to emulate the method of tune changing used on cylinder boxes, for with two sets of projections on each disc it was possible to change the tune by moving the centre spindle up or down slightly into either of two positions. The Sirion was made by a small firm in Germany at the turn of the century and is extremely rare. I know only of two in America and one in Germany. It would be interesting to hear where the others are.

The Komet

Another great rarity, not unlike Halley's comet which comes round every seventy-five years. I have seen two so far and feel it is unlikely that there are many more in existence. One was in a dealer's shop and was similar to a $19\frac{1}{8}$ in. upright Polyphon, but didn't play nearly as well. The other really was a magnificent machine. Many remember well the day the Komet came to the Portobello Road. Set in a huge cabinet was a movement which played a $33\frac{5}{8}$ in. disc, one of the largest ever made. 198 steel teeth on an assembly of ten steel combs played the music, part of which was arranged for fourteen tuned bells. The bells were struck with butterfly strikers. Truly a once-in-a-lifetime machine.

The Capital Cuff Box

When Brackhausen was starting up his business in Rahway, he lived in a house in Jersey City which was across the road from a man called Frederick Otto, a manufacturer of surgical instruments. It is quite likely that Otto knew Brackhausen well, and mellowed with a glass or two of Schnapps was repeatedly told of the success of the Regina Factory in Rahway. It is part of human nature to want to emulate the success of another and so it was not long before

Otto had put one of his machinists in charge of designing a music box. In 1894 he filed a patent for a musical box with the usual comb, but instead of the disc tune sheet, a conical-shaped note-barrel was designed. Because of the resemblance of the note-barrel to a starched cuff the name "Capital Cuff Box" was born. The spring of the mechanism was also quite radical in design. Instead of a spiral spring contained in a barrel the motive force was obtained from a set of elliptical springs. They are all pushed up to one end of the case and it is their tendency to distribute themselves right across the length of the case which provides the motive force. The Capital Cuff Box was good in tone and robust in design, but apart from the fact that the cuff tune sheets could be stacked one inside the other and kept inside the box there was little advantage over other makes. They were made for a comparatively short time. Records show that they started in 1894 and were being produced in 1897, but there is no record of when manufacture ceased. It is virtually impossible to find one in Europe since few were exported from the States.

The Tune Sheets

The metal discs or tune sheets were nearly always made of either zinc or steel. Zinc was easier to work, and so the projections could be stamped from zinc discs with less damage to the punches. However they did not last nearly as long as steel discs and the projections were much more prone to break off. Also zinc was more expensive.

Throughout this chapter I have classified the machines by the size of disc which they play, quoting the diameter in inches. This measurement is critical since practically no disc is interchangeable from make to make. The 15½ in. Polyphon disc will fit the 15½ in. Regina machine but apart from that each machine will play only the discs made for it. Not only does the diameter of the disc differ from make to make, but also there are changes in the register of the combs and in the method of drive of the disc. The Polyphons of 15½ in. and larger drive the disc by means of round holes at the edge,

but the Symphonion is driven from the centre, where it is slipped over two projecting drive pins.

The tune sheets were originally made from masters in a hydraulic press. The operator would place a guide into the hole in the master disc and then depress a lever with his foot. The press would come down to make a projection in the desired place. Multiple presses arranged in layers would turn out more than one disc at a time. In this way literally thousands of discs were produced, but it is quite extraordinary that today only one of the original disc-stamping machines exists as far as we know. Owned by an American collector, it is one of those used by the Regina Company for making 15½ in. discs and has about two hundred masters with it.

But all is not lost, because one sunny day in Muswell Hill an English enthusiast with above-average mechanical ingenuity was given a short bedplate Regina 15½ in. table model. Unfortunately he had no discs and could find no one willing to sell him any. He was shown a rough sketch of the Regina disc-stamping machine and many sleepless nights and one thousand seven hundred hours later another machine had been made. It is capable of copying existing discs of any size between 12 in. and 24 in. and can produce the projections and register for almost every disc music box. Its versatility is much greater than the original and it has been put to good use making high quality discs out of tinplate. Not content with copying the old, the same man has set up at least two pieces of modern music on 15½ in. discs for his Regina so it is now possible to hear contemporary music played on a musical box made many years before it was written. There are many people who talk about the possibilities of producing discs and so on, but it is reassuring to know that there are some who will actually carry out their theories.

Musical Clocks

For the most part, disc boxes are not particularly decorative, the cases being of heavy design with a surfeit of ornate Victorian

carving. Because they were primarily functional objects rather than ornaments the market could have been limited to those who were music lovers, but Polyphon captured a larger market by making grandfather clocks which contained a music box. They were advertised as Polyphon Hall Clocks and were most suitable for large Edwardian houses. The music box was contained in the case of the clock, disc sizes usually being 11 in. or $15\frac{1}{2}$ in. The music could be set off at the hour by the clock. The Polyphon Hall Clocks were often as tall as nine feet but smaller models were made by the Symphonion Company, who incorporated $11\frac{3}{4}$ in. and $13\frac{1}{2}$ in. disc movements in the clocks. Symphonion also made a splendid little wooden alarm clock, which has a $4\frac{1}{2}$ in. movement in the top of the case.

Buying a Disc Machine

There are several points to observe when you are buying a disc machine. The most important of these is the obvious one—the number of discs available. If you are offered a disc music box without many discs it is as well to know that the discs of Polyphons and Symphonions are virtually the only ones that can be obtained readily. So don't buy a Fortuna machine without discs, unless you know someone who will lend you discs of his own to be copied. The chances of finding Fortuna discs on the open market are practically nil.

After you have inspected the combs, and it is very easy to detect damage to these, make quite sure that the lead resonators on them are intact. They are hidden under the teeth and hard to see, but are often bent so that they touch one another and so cannot vibrate. Lead is also subject to sulphating, a chemical ageing process which causes it to powder away. A comb without resonators has no bass notes, sounds most out of tune and is hard to repair.

The dampers can also spoil the quality of a box but you will not be able to tell whether they are in good adjustment or not until you have played a disc. So play the machine and listen for the tell-tale

squeaks. Dampers can be replaced on Symphonions, Polyphons and Reginas but it would be difficult to replace broken dampers on other makes.

As you will read in Chapter 8, the clockwork mechanism of a disc box can be repaired quite readily, so don't be put off a purchase because of a fault in the mechanism.

Many people think the disc music box makes the finest sound of all musical boxes. This could be true, but they do seem to lack the individuality of musical arrangement found on a cylinder machine. Whatever your opinion may be, they certainly represent an interesting stage towards the development of the gramophone.

5

Musical Objets d'Art

The traveller to Dubrovnik will find not only the oldest pharmacy in the world—it was in use in 1317—but he will also visit the market where it is possible to buy the products of the local pottery, including little whistles made of clay which can be filled with water, so that as you blow they bubble to imitate the song of a bird. Throughout history man has tried to imitate birdsong by mechanical means; for example, in China there was an emperor who had a pet nightingale, favourite in the palace until a mechanical bird was presented by envoys from Japan. The mechanical bird was made of silver and jewels and soon the drab nightingale was banished from the land. Unfortunately, however, the mechanism failed and the bird stopped singing, much to the dismay of the court, and the emperor was so upset by it all that he became seriously ill. There was a happy ending to the fable however, when the real nightingale returned to sing by the bedside of the emperor, reviving him and regaining its own position in the palace.

The clockwork bird given to the emperor may well have been of Swiss origin, one of the masterpieces made in that country between 1770 and the present day. It is thought by Alfred Chapuis that the invention of the singing-bird snuffbox was made either by Pierre Jaquet-Droz or Jean Frédérick Leschot or as a result of collaboration between them. They began an industry which flourished until about 1850, when bird boxes continued to be made, but with a noticeable drop in quality. Singing-bird boxes display all the skills of the watchmaker's craft but there were no more than half a dozen or so better-known makers who marketed them in any quantity before

French Ormolu mantel clock by Henri Robert of Paris,
c. 1835. The oval base contains a musical movement

Three musical snuff boxes all made about 1840: *left*, composition inlaid with mother-of-pearl and silver containing a movement by Nicole Frères; *bottom*, tortoiseshell box containing a movement by M. Bordier; *bottom right*, moulded tortoiseshell box containing a movement by Henri Lecoultre

Delicate boxwood and satinwood inlay on a rosewood-veneered key-wind box by François Lecoultre, *c.* 1850

Above, forte-piano box by Nicole Frères, No. 30032, *c.* 1850;
below, interior of a mandoline box by David Lecoultre, *c.* 1850

Mandoline forte-piano box by Langdorf et Fils, *c.* 1860; *below,* Czechoslovakian movement by Willembacher and Rzebitschek, Prague, *c.* 1850

mass-production came in 1850. They took a long time to make and so compared with other items comparatively few exist and they seldom come up for sale. They were expensive items when new and were often cased in precious metal decorated with enamels and semi-precious or precious stones.

The mechanism of the singing-bird snuffbox is perhaps the finest and most complicated that a collector will come across. On sliding a button on the front of the box to one side the oval lid lifts up to display a mechanical bird no more than an inch long. Accompanied by its song, the bird flaps its wings and also makes independent movements of its head, beak and tail. When the song is over, the bird drops back into the box and the lid is closed over it. The tiny birds are decorated with iridescent humming bird feathers, and move in a most lifelike way. The early Swiss bird boxes are fusee wind and this point of identification will serve to distinguish them from the later inferior boxes. The winding square is situated well in one corner of the underside of the box and is often wound with a male key, anti-clockwise. The clockwork drives bellows which are usually made from steel covered with special thin parchment known as "zephyr skin", and the air from the bellows plays a whistle whose note is altered by a moving plunger. The other main part of the mechanism is a set of five rotating cams; first there is a cam which is shaped to control the notes of the song of the bird by moving the piston backwards and forwards in the whistle; secondly the song is stopped and started with an air valve controlled by another cam, which also moves the beak and tail of the bird; a third cam controls the side-to-side movement of the bird's head and a fourth opens and closes its wings; the fifth cam is shaped to make the bird turn on its perch.

The first two cams are the key to the quality of the song of the bird and by a correct co-ordination of the air valve and the piston it is possible to imitate the song of the nightingale or blackbird. These cams are usually made in sets of three or four so that the variety of the song can be extended beyond a single revolution by bringing

E

65

each set into play in turn. Great diligence went into the design of the song cams and their shape was usually planned with the aid of a musical score. They were moved from set to set by means of a snail in just the same way that the tune of a cylinder music box is changed.

The quality of the work that went into the construction of an early Swiss bird box is apparent by the finish which was always given to the component parts of the mechanism. The levers were made of steel and were usually given a high polish and temper. Later move-movements had levers made of brass which were easier to make but which soon showed signs of wear and often bent out of their original shape. On the later boxes the lid was allowed to drop down at the end of the song; it was a matter of touch-and-go for the poor bird whether he got his head down in time and you will see many with bald patches on top because they were not quick enough. The Swiss makers got over this by delaying the lid to give the bird time to drop into the box first. A separate wheel train controls the speed at which the lid is lowered; this of course put up the price of the box and was one of the first things to be left out of the cheaper variety.

There are certain makers of early singing bird boxes who are worth looking for but, as with many other music boxes and auto-mata, they did not always make their work apparent by signing it. The earliest and perhaps most sought after is Pierre Jaquet-Droz and we are lucky in that he often did engrave the movement with his name. Work by him, however, is extremely rare, and you would have to pay several thousands of pounds to buy one of his bird boxes in auction.

Working with Droz was Jean Frédérick Leschot and it is unusual to find a bird box made by him since, until the death of Jaquet-Droz in 1791, all Leschot's work bore the other's name. The firm was situated in Geneva and London.

Jacob Frisard was born at Villaret in the Jura in 1753 and worked with Leschot until about 1800 when he started working on his own account. He spent much of his time in Vienna but also lived in London and Geneva, and specialized in fitting singing-bird mecha-

nisms into *objets d'art* such as scent bottles. A fine example of his work is a gold and enamel fruit basket, the lid of which is decorated with half pearls. When the lid is opened a singing bird rises from the bed of enamelled fruits.

An important competitor of Jaquet-Droz was Henry Maillardet who went into business in about 1791. He was in the habit of sub-contracting much of his work and used to send many of the song cams of his bird boxes to Frisard for cutting. Nevertheless he was a great rival of Jaquet-Droz and made many fine pieces.

So far nothing has been said of the construction of the bird itself, and it is hard to believe that these masterpieces of the watchmaker's craft, often only 15 mm. from beak to tail, consisted of up to forty separate components. The body was made in two halves, to which were attached the head, tail and wings, with an internal mechanism so that all the parts could be moved independently. The tiny birds were dressed with humming bird feathers and the work was of great skill. Many of the makers used to send the birds to a specialist in feathering called Sandoz who worked in Geneva with his wife, finishing the birds with the brilliant plumage of humming birds and kingfishers. Not only was their work most skilful but it was also extremely difficult to make a collection of feathers which were small enough for the job.

Among the most prolific makers of the early high quality bird boxes was the firm of Rochat Frères, whose work is most sought after by collectors. The firm existed between 1804 and 1825 in Switzerland. D. Rochat et Fils worked for Jaquet-Droz and Leschot before working on their own account in 1804 at Le Brassus, and later the firm of Rochat Frères was established at Geneva, in 1810. Many singing birds of the highest quality were made by them and quite the most extraordinary of these are three singing-bird pistols. Made of gold and decorated with the finest quality enamels they are probably three of the most expensive toys ever made. Rochat adapted the design of the mechanism of the singing-bird box so that it would fit into a double-barrelled pistol about 6½ in. long, and in

so doing set himself an almost impossible task. However, three pistols were made and two are still working today. The mechanism is wound by cocking the hammer. On pulling the trigger, a tiny bird, smaller than most singing birds, appears from the end of the barrels to sing and move until the mechanism runs down. The bird then finishes its song and moves back into the barrel of the pistol. The first constructional problem which must have been posed for Rochat was to transmit all the controls for the movements of the bird up the entire length of the barrel. It took great ingenuity to do this. The two surviving pistols are marked with the initials FR in an oval, the Rochat trade mark. One is in the Salomon collection in this country, the second is in Paris, but the third, alas, is lost. It will I hope be found by a collector and restored to the condition of the other two.

Rochat Frères also made a great number of normal bird boxes, of which a large number can be identified by the trade mark on the movement. Many of their birds were bigger than usual and the grill through which they appeared would not usually be pierced to the extent of those of other makers. Rochat singing birds often had four sets of song cams played in a simple sequence A, B, C, and D, unlike those of other makers.

Perhaps the birds that the collector is most likely to come across are by Bruguier, a Geneva family. Charles Abraham Bruguier was born in Geneva in 1788 and during his lifetime was, with the assistance of his two sons responsible for the manufacture of a great number of singing birds. Unlike Rochat, who made no cuts in the quality of his bird boxes, Bruguier began to think in terms of large scale production, and although the quality of his work is good you will find that he has often made economies in the finish in order to lower the cost. The song of a Bruguier bird, however, is very good and there are many who prefer it to that produced by Rochat. Usually four sets of cams are used and in this case three of the cams are played twice, the sequence being A, A, B, C, B, C, and D. As can be seen the song is far longer and more elaborate than that of

Three fine singing-bird boxes: *left*, silver and enamel bird box by Charles Bruguier of Geneva, *c.* 1830; *centre*, unusually small and rare tortoiseshell bird box with enamel lid. German, *c.* 1890; *right*, modern silver and enamel bird box by Greisbaum of Germany

Rochat. Charles Bruguier was also an important repairer of singing birds and other automata and his name is often seen scratched on the mechanism of other makes. He died in 1862 leaving the business to his two sons and grandson.

After about 1850 the quality of singing-bird boxes was reduced and they were produced on a much larger scale. The levers in the mechanism were made of brass which was much more easy to work, but which could also easily bend out of true. The bird itself no longer could turn its head from side to side and the lid was allowed to fall back into place at the end of the song without the control of a separate train of wheels. Quite the most remarkable piece of standardisation which occurred, however, was that all of these later bird boxes play the same song. This would seem to imply that all the song cams were cut in the same workshop.

The collector can be led sadly astray when he is buying a singing-bird box and can easily pay an antique price for a new article. The cheaper variety of bird box has been made from about 1850 right up to the present day and it is sometimes quite difficult to date one accurately. The bird no longer turns its head from side to side, and the clockwork mechanism is no longer fusee, but after 1850 few other changes were made to the mechanism. The birds until about 1900 usually had a beak made from bone or ivory, but after that date it was nearly always made from metal. At about the same date the quality of the grill through which the bird lifts also changed. The earlier grills were pierced with hand files and then engraved and gilded, but the later grills were simply pressed out of brass before being gilded. Clues to the age of the case of a singing-bird box are given by the materials used—any evidence of the use of synthetic resins or plastics betrays it as a modern piece—and the date marks on the case if it is made of precious metal. Since the 1950s the firm of Carl Greisbaum in the Black Forest have made quantities of very good quality singing-bird boxes in all types of finish including enamel and it is quite difficult to distinguish them from an antique. These recent mechanisms, however, employ the use of nylon for the

last wheel in the train, nylon being ideal since it is very hard and self-lubricating.

Restoration of Singing-Bird Boxes

All work carried out on a complicated mechanism takes a long time and so will be very expensive. Since the early bird boxes were all hand made there is virtually nothing which cannot be remade and replaced, but it is very difficult to find someone who is capable of doing the work competently, so view the possible purchase of a broken bird box with scepticism. You may well have to lay out more for the repair work than for the original purchase, and the repair work could take a year—if you are lucky enough to find someone who will do it for you.

Musical Seals

An item of musical jewellery which it is relatively easy to buy is the musical seal. There usually seems to be one or two on the market in London for those who are willing to pay the price. This is probably because they are quite expensive and the music you get for a relatively large outlay is often very poor. I have seen few seals which play any sort of recognisable melody, but many that make only a meaningless tinkle. The musical movement is usually of the earliest type, namely Favre's original laminated stack of teeth plucked by pins in the spring barrel. In most instances this limits the music to about eight notes or so and only the simplest airs can be attempted. Musical seals are nearly always made of gold and often decorated with enamel and hard stones.

Unfortunately, seals are often faked because of the high prices they can fetch. It is possible to take out the stone from a large antique fob seal, insert one of the tiny modern musical movements which can be bought and cover the base again with a thin sheet of gold. Such work is child's play to a competent jeweller. I have seen one such seal being offered as an antique playing *Deep in the Heart of Texas*. The forger's knowledge of music obviously did not come

up to his manual skill. If you have any doubts about buying a musical seal, look very carefully at the stop-start slide. If the seal is a fake you can usually see that the hole for the slide is cut rather crudely in the gold. Also it is as well to inspect the movement. A modern mechanism is easy to detect and is of the comb and cylinder type; the seal must contain either the laminated stack type of movement, or the radial disc type.

Musical Watches

Musical watches were made as toys for the show-off, whose embroidered silk waistcoat in the Regency period would contain in its pocket silk handkerchiefs, gold chains, vinaigrettes and snuff-boxes; but in certain cases all these accoutrements would be topped with a musical watch. Such a curiosity would enable you to win easy popularity from your grandchildren or to be "one up" over competitive suitors for a fair lady's hand.

As we have seen the first musical movements were made by watchmakers and so it is not surprising that they soon incorporated both skills by making a musical watch. Philippe Samuel Meylan made the first watch to contain a radial-disc-type movement, since that was fairly easy to fit into a slim watch case. Most of these watches are quarter-repeaters as well as being musical, and so they contain three trains of wheels, one for the timepiece, one for the repeat mechanism and one for the music. The music train has a separate spring barrel and winding mechanism, and the repeat work is activated by depressing the stem of the watch. The music played is much more ambitious than that of the musical seal, since about thirty notes are either side of the disc. Most musical watches seem to play one of the popular Swiss traditional airs *Ranz des Vaches*, but occasionally you will find other melodies including the National Anthems of both England and France. I have also recently heard *Rule Britannia* played by a watch. Operatic airs are sometimes heard on watches but only on those of the better makers.

Musical watches were made by Le Roy of Paris, Henri Capt of

Geneva, Dubois of La Chaux-de-Fonds, Jean Antoine Lepine of Paris and Piguet et Meylan of Geneva. There also seems to be a large number of unnamed ones about of inferior quality, and so the collector is advised to wait until he has the opportunity of buying a really good musical watch. There are many which are poorly finished and for which you will probably have to pay just as much.

Some musical watches were made with comb and cylinder movements. These were difficult to make and so they are quite rare compared with the disc type of movement. There is not much to choose between the quality of the music but perhaps the comb and cylinder type does give slightly more resonance. Musical watches are difficult and expensive to have repaired, and so they require extra close inspection prior to buying. The watch escapement is usually a cylinder, and if the cylinder is broken it will be doubly hard to replace, since for some reason the escape wheel of a musical watch nearly always revolves anti-clockwise making a left-handed cylinder necessary. The repeat works often break and the parts are difficult to make and replace. Sometimes the repeat works strike too fast. This is because of wrong adjustment or a missing pinion and should not put you off the purchase. Finally you should inspect the trip mechanism for the musical train. It consists of hand-made parts which will be expensive to replace. If the music train runs, its speed can be adjusted without much difficulty. Last of all, watches are subject to recasing. Often the gold case was melted down by the original owner or his family and the watch was replaced in a cheaper silver case. As long as this has been done so that it does not show, the value of the watch will not be affected too much, but if the case is obviously wrong then the value will be reduced by half or more.

Early Carillon and Automaton Boxes

If you are ever lucky enough to find a small musical box which plays on bells instead of steel teeth, it will probably be extremely early. Very few such boxes appear on the open market and one of the most recent, an enamelled gold box containing a carillon musical

movement, fetched several thousands of pounds in the salerooms. When the music is started, two doors on top of the box open to display a scene in a music room in which tiny automata are moving. One plays the harpsichord, another plays a harp while a third taps his foot to the music. The whole box is decorated with guilloche green enamel panels, and on either side of the two doors are panels which depict the goddess of dancing and the goddess of music.

While some of these automaton boxes show musical scenes, there are others which depict a variety of animated figures, some of which tell your fortune. The fortune-teller points to an opening in which one of several possible influences on your future will appear.

Watches with Singing Birds and Barking Dogs

Perhaps the rarest of all of these masterpieces are the few watches containing either a singing bird or a barking dog. The former contain all the mechanism of the singing bird in addition to the normal watch mechanism, and when a lever is pressed the bird appears either out of the side of the watch or out of its back to sing a life-like song. The barking dog repeater watch is a rare and much desired collector's item. Instead of having a strike the watch displays an animated dog which barks the hours and quarters.

Finally we come to watches that display moving tableaux, which if made today would infringe the laws of obscenity. The Regency imagination was as liberal if not more so than that of the Cairo postcard-seller, but the scenes depicted in such watches certainly display much finer workmanship. All the artistry of Swiss watch-making and enamelling come to the rescue of what would otherwise cause offence to the more prudish.

6

Other Forms of Mechanical Music

It is not always appreciated that cylinder and disc music boxes are about the only form of mechanical music which are not merely a mechanised version of an ordinary musical instrument. When the tuned steel comb was invented, a new form of instrument was born which could be played only by mechanical means. The nearest relative in the symphony orchestra is the dulcitone which consists of a set of tuning forks struck with hammers controlled from a keyboard. The dulcitone makes a very soft sound and is not often used in the orchestra; the louder celesta usually takes its place.

The Chamber Barrel Organ

In Chapter 1 we saw that the first instrument to be mechanised was the pipe organ, a pinned barrel taking the place of the musician. After about 1750 the centre of the barrel organ industry was England where many were made, mostly in London. In the eighteenth century they were the only form of mechanical music available to the public apart from carillon clocks, and so they became extremely popular items of furniture in the home. Cased in elegant mahogany cabinets the front of which would be decorated with a set of gilt dummy organ pipes, they played an average of thirty tunes on three barrels of ten each. The music was usually sacred, Scottish or popular dance, and the instruments must have often been used to accompany family prayers and parties. Some of the larger chamber organs would

German street pipe organ, made about 1870

have a drum and triangle accompaniment, to accentuate the rhythm so that they were more suitable for the dance in a crowded room.

It is still possible to find these fine instruments, although the ravages of woodworm has made them quite rare. Before the days of modern chemistry, a piece of furniture affected by woodworm was burned to prevent the parasite spreading, but now a good application of any well-known woodworm killer will affect a complete cure. Having cured the worm, however, you will find that a great deal of work will be necessary to make the pneumatics of the organ efficient again. All the worm holes have to be stopped and usually the bellows have to be re-covered with new leather. Barrel organs are for the dedicated collector, who is not afraid of work. There are certain makers worth keeping an eye open for and these are: Flight and Robson of St Martin's Lane; Bryceson Brothers; Astor and Horwood; Fentum; Clementi; Longman and Broderip; T. C. Bates; J. C. Bishop and J. W. Walker.

Bird Organs

A very small type of barrel organ was used to teach pet canaries to sing. About six inches square, they contained a single rank of high-pitched pipes on which a simple tune that the bird could easily mimic was played by turning a handle. In the collection at the Paris Conservatoire there is a bird organ in the shape of a book, on the spine of which is the title *L'Art d'Élever les Serins* or "The Art of Teaching Canaries". Bird organs are often known as "Serinettes", or occasionally as "Merlines" when a blackbird or "Merle" was to receive the lesson. The Serinette in Paris dates back to 1765. Items as old as that are naturally very rare, but in the nineteenth century the Serinette developed into a barrel organ in miniature which could play a few popular melodies instead of the bird song, and it is possible to find a few of these small organs still for sale. They do not usually play very well, but are interesting items for a collection.

Italian Street Organs

The Italian organ grinder with his monkey usually played a development of the Serinette supported on a pole so that its weight was taken off his shoulders while it was played. Although the streets in the nineteenth century were a great deal quieter than they are today, there was still a fair amount of clatter going on so it was imperative that the street organ should play loud music. The earlier ones played on pipes but later on they were nearly all reed organs which played the popular airs of the time; traditional songs, operatic arias and Viennese waltzes with their familiar "Oom-Pa-Pa" bass accompaniment were frequently heard. I had a strong desire some time ago to own one of these organs and finally found one in fair condition in an antique shop in Oxford. The pneumatics were in fairly good order but the barrel was badly out of register. The only way to register this type of organ is by trial and error, since there is no adjusting screw; the whole instrument had to be screwed into the wooden case in different positions until I had got it right. It took a very long time, since when the organ was in the case it was not possible to see which way the error lay. The outcome was that after very many trial attempts I finally found the correct register, but only after the entire neighbourhood had become heartily sick of the sound of the instrument. Even I found that the music had lost its initial charm and exchanged the organ for a musical snuffbox which plays beautifully and occupies an important place in my collection.

Italian organs were a common sight in London until the mid-1930s when the organ grinders mostly returned to Italy, having been offered a more promising future by Mussolini. By that time also there was legislation in this country which described them as "public nuisances" and restricted their activities.

Barrel Pianos

Henry VIII is said to have owned a virginal which had been mechanised so that it played music from a pinned barrel. That was

prior to his death in 1547, but the collector today is far more likely to find a barrel piano developed from the invention of Joseph Hicks in the early nineteenth century. He made an upright pianoforte which was played with a pinned barrel, and it was not long before many such instruments were to be seen in England. A large number were supplied with a hand-cart so that they could be played and wheeled through the streets of our cities.

My first memories of London are St Pancras railway station where we disembarked after our journey south. I can also clearly remember hearing a street barrel piano outside my grandmother's house in Swiss Cottage. These street barrel pianos, often called barrel organs incorrectly, were made for use indoors also, sometimes very tastefully housed in beautifully inlaid cabinets. Penny-in-the-slot operation is frequently found. It is fairly easy to find a barrel piano for your collection as there are many on the market, but it will be difficult to find one that plays well and which is not loud and brash when heard in your living-room.

Earlier than the large street barrel piano is a smaller version which was carried on the shoulders of the musician. Standing about three feet high these small instruments usually play about six airs and are extremely difficult to keep in tune since they are strung on a wooden frame.

Barrel Orchestrions

The ultimate in barrel instruments is the orchestrion. Most familiar of these is the fairground organ, many of which were originally made to play music which was pinned onto wooden barrels, although they have now mostly been converted to play music from perforated books. The orchestrion was made by Imhof and Muckle in 1860. They designed and constructed a barrel organ of large proportions which played music pinned spirally on to rosewood barrels 28 in. long. The music is played on 85 wooden pipes divided into two stops with the bottom ten pipes being shared by both. The two stops differ in volume. The music from such a machine is really

magnificent, but a word of caution to the collector; the orchestrion stands about seven feet high and the works are driven by a weight which weighs close on one-third of a ton. I have honestly heard a case reported where the orchestrion started on the first-floor landing and found its way to the hall during the night through an enormous hole in the ceiling.

Imhof and Muckle orchestrions are relatively simple in construction compared with the fairground organ which sometimes reaches giant proportions. These mammoth orchestrions were used in the fairground to attract visitors to the "Bioscope" or moving picture show, and the competition between them led to the construction of really mighty instruments. Perhaps the largest fair organ ever built was made by Gavioli in 1908 in Paris, and delivered to South Wales in the following year to join Sidney White's Electric Coliseum Bioscope and Variety Show. It is a 112-note instrument which has available a dozen or so stops or ranks of pipes, and was in constant use until 1939 when the war caused it to be silent. In 1954 it was dismantled prior to being destroyed but luckily an ardent collector and mechanical music enthusiast, George Parmley of County Durham, rescued the organ and restored it to its original condition with the assistance of some of his friends. He is a collector obviously undaunted by size, for the organ has been completely rebuilt and its elaborate gilded decoration fully restored. Recordings have been made of it and are available on the Decca Label.

The Music Roll

One of the most important developments in the production of mechanical music was due to the invention of the perforated paper roll for the reproduction of a musical score. This was made possible when the pneumatic lever became a feasible alternative for the mechanical tracker action of the barrel organ. First tried in 1827, it was soon found that a perforated sheet of cardboard or paper was a suitable alternative to the pinned barrel for the control of the notes. Patents were taken out in France and England in the 1840s but it

was not until 1878 that the paper roll Organette was made. This is a small chamber reed organ, turned by hand, through which passes a long perforated sheet of paper on which the music is scored. Many such Organettes were produced and they are fairly easy to come by. The better-known makes are the Mignon, Celestina and Seraphone.

The Welte-Mignon Orchestrion

In 1887, Emil Welte of the Welte-Mignon Company at Freiburg-im-Breisgan patented a pneumatic paper roll action for use with either pianos or organs, and his invention led to the manufacture of a number of fine orchestrions, which were designed to be used in large houses or assembly-rooms. The collector can still find these magnificent machines for sale, but since the smallest are about eight feet high a certain amount of reorganisation would be necessary before bringing one home. A typical Welte orchestrion has forty-four notes which play on eight stops or ranks of pipes with the addition of a percussion section; triangle, snare drum and bass drum. The music played by these instruments is largely operatic, but selections of marches and popular melodies are also to be found.

The Pianola

Soon after the advent of the paper roll for the mechanical reproduction of music came the invention of the player piano. In 1897 an American, Mr E. S. Votey, constructed a contrivance that could be pushed up to the keyboard of an ordinary piano. Felt-covered fingers projected from the front and these played the keys of the piano when activated by a perforated paper roll. This push-up device was improved so that its mechanism became built into the piano to make the pianola as we know it today.

The early pianolas controlled only 66 notes in the middle of the keyboard, but later 88-note models came out. Expression in the music was controlled by the operator who could change the pressure of air pumped into the pneumatics of the pianola. The air was supplied from bellows worked by the feet of the operator.

The greatest advance in the development of pianolas was the introduction of the reproducing piano. Similar in appearance to the earlier models, these machines reproduced all the expression required in the music without any manual control being necessary. Extra rows of perforations on the paper roll were able to give individual volume and pedal control to particular areas of the keyboard. The music played by a well-adjusted reproducing piano is very close in every way to the original performance of the pianist. In this way many famous names such as Cortot, Paderewski, and Busoni have been permanently recorded on paper rolls and their performances can be heard with an accuracy of which the early phonograph was not capable. The best reproducing pianos were made by: Welte-Mignon, Ampico (American Piano Company), Duo-Art (Aeolian Company), and Steck.

The Aeolian Orchestrelle

At the turn of the century the Aeolian Company of New Bond Street were producing a large variety of paper roll organs which were designed to be played at home. Like the Welte organs they are rather too large to be accommodated by most modern houses, but if you do have room for such an instrument you will have at your command all the music and tones of a real church organ. The Aeolian Company managed to make reed organs which gave a range of tonality covering the majority of pipe organ stops. It must have been difficult to design a reed with a resonator to sound like a flute, but they achieved this with great success.

To play an orchestrelle is quite an experience. Unlike the pianola, when all you have to do is work the pedals, the orchestrelle allows the player to choose the stops of his own choice, and so entirely different interpretations can be made of a single piece of music. Puccini is reported to have said, "With an Aeolian Orchestrelle all who do not know a note of music, but who are gifted with a refined musical taste, can readily become familiar with what is most elevat-

Automaton monkey violinist with musical movement in the oval base, *c.* 1860

French Poupée musical doll, *c.* 1860

Above, a fine pair of French automaton musical dolls, *c.* 1865;
below, case of Grande Format Overture Box by Nicole Frères.
No. 46,000 series, *c.* 1865

ing in the musical art. The Aeolian Orchestrelle, however, is to music what a vast encyclopedia is to science."

It certainly was possible to equip yourself with an enormous repertoire of music for the orchestrelle and buy music rolls of almost any type to suit any taste. Favourite rolls of mine are the overture to Mendelssohn's *Midsummer Night's Dream* and selections from Lecoq's opera, *La Fille de Madame Angot*. It is also possible for you to perform the New World Symphony of Dvořak and the Archduke Trio of Beethoven. The feeling of power while sitting at the keyboard of an Orchestrelle is indescribable.

The Violino Virtuoso

Virtually any musical instrument can be mechanised and it was not long before a violin had played music from a paper roll. During the first half of this century the Mills Novelty Company were marketing a musical machine which represented a violin with piano accompaniment played from a paper roll. The piano presented no more difficulties than the pianola, but the violin was made specially so that the strings could be stopped pneumatically at the desired place on the finger board. The bow of the instrument was circular and rotated round the body of the violin. At first it was difficult to produce anything other than glissando notes but it was soon found that staccato music could be played by reversing the direction of rotation of the circular bow for each note. The mechanical violin was taken to its extreme by the Hupfeld Company in Germany, who made a complete mechanical string quartet.

The Tanzbar Mechanical Accordion

The accordion was the invention of Buschmann of Berlin in 1822, and it was not long before attempts were being made to mechanise it so that it could play music from paper rolls or barrels. The Tanzbar mechanical accordion was designed to play from paper rolls and was the result of a German patent of the 1890s. The music roll is pulled over a set of levers by an inertia motor set in motion when a hand

lever is pumped. When a lever is allowed to protrude through a hole in the roll the respective note is sounded. The instrument has the appearance of a normal accordion with the mechanics in one end. Incidentally "Tanzbar" is an adaptation of the German for "dancing bear".

Mechanised Banjo and Zither

The Wurlitzer Company of America produced a mechanical banjo which played paper roll music and made a particularly raucous noise. The construction, however, was clever and in addition to the controls on the finger board which stopped the strings where required there was an ingenious quadruple strumming mechanism which could play strings individually or together.

Far more pleasant to the ear is the "Triola" mandolin zither which combines mechanical reproduction with hand operation. A zither is fitted with a mechanism activated by turning a handle, which causes vibrating fingers to strum the strings. In this fashion the melody is produced from a paper roll while the bass accompaniment is played by hand or plectrum by plucking the appropriate chord. The instruments are rare and were made in America from 1894 when the patent was taken out.

Cardboard Book Music

The paper roll was a very convenient way of storing a music score, but it was prone to damage by tearing. A stronger music sheet could be made out of cardboard, folded into the form of a book instead of being rolled up. This book music was used and still is being used on street orchestrions, which need a robust music sheet. Anyone who has been to Holland and seen their splendid "Draaiorgels" playing in Amsterdam must have seen the books of music passed through the organ.

A rare instrument which plays from book music is the Racca piano. Made in Italy by Giovanni Racca in 1886, it has the outward appearance of a grand piano in miniature but an arrangement as wide

as the keyboard allows book music to pass through the machine and control the melody. Rather than play simple notes the instrument was designed to play with a tremolo effect, and this gives it a most romantic sound. Racca himself must have been a great lover of Puccini, because the majority of the music books for his "Piano Melodico" are of music by this composer.

Cardboard Discs

Some of the first organettes were played with cardboard discs instead of paper rolls, which were introduced to improve on the playing time available during the revolution of a disc. The Ariston was one of the earliest. It was the product of the Ehrlich brothers who also produced the Monopol disc music box. Ariston machines usually seem to be on the market, possibly because it isn't often that you find one which plays really well: many of them have leaks in the pneumatics which can lead to hours of trying work for a collector. The Orpheus disc piano also plays music scored on a perforated cardboard disc. It is a rare instrument and looks like a tiny grand piano.

Every day new finds are being made and new mechanical musical instruments are being found. Never be put off buying if you find a machine which is not recorded in any book. It is always possible that you have rediscovered some instrument of which all traces have been previously lost.

7

Automata

Your collection should not be limited to musical boxes alone: there is a lot of satisfaction to be gained from collecting automata, some of which contain musical movements. Those which are silent will still add colour to your collection.

Vaucanson's Duck

Jacques Vaucanson was born in Grenoble in 1709, the tenth son of a family of glovemakers, and at an early age exhibited a gift for the design and construction of automaton figures. He came to Paris at the age of 26, and like many men of that time was fascinated with the idea of being able to reproduce life artificially. In this he was not successful, and was able to make only a few "moving anatomies" which were not completed due to lack of funds. The experience gained by this compelled him to devote his efforts to something which would be slightly more lucrative, and so he began to design figures for public exhibition. The most celebrated of all of them was a famous duck which was remarkable in its mimicry of a real bird. In his prospectus Vaucanson says, "An artificial duck made of gilded copper who drinks, eats, quacks, splashes about on the water, and digests his food like a living duck." Feathers were attached to the framework of the duck so that they all behaved exactly as they would do on a living bird throughout the complicated movements it performed. The silken skin was covered with down, which in turn was covered with larger feathers whose movements could be controlled by the mechanism. The wings were equipped with feathers of the correct size so that when they were opened and closed it was

often doubtful to the audience whether the duck would actually take off in flight or not. The tail was made up of about twenty feathers, each hinged separately so that the tail could open and close rapidly and smoothly.

Monsieur Vaucanson would walk up to the duck which stood upon a large pedestal and touch a feather in the upper part of the bird. It would raise its head, look about, stretch itself and flap its wings, making a perfectly natural noise. After a few of these movements the duck would bend over and swallow a plateful of grain in the most lifelike manner, and now the previous experience of Vaucanson with moving anatomies came to the fore. The food was actually digested and finally excreted, by which time most of the audience must have forgotten the mechanical origin of the bird.

The duck travelled over much of France. From Lyons to Valence, through the Rhône Valley to Avignon, and finally to Marseilles. There is a record of the show at Avignon from a letter which says, "On Sunday night there was a crowd, a queue formed and there were no vacant seats. After each of the duck's performances there was an interval of a quarter of an hour to replace the food. A singer announced the duck. As soon as the audience saw it climbing on to the stage, everybody cried 'Quack, quack, quack.' Greatest amazement was caused when it drank three glasses of wine, filling everyone with wonder."

The history of the duck, recounted in some detail in Chapuis and Droz's *Automata*, is not only interesting from the mechanical point of view but also for its ownership. It was completed in 1738 and shown in Paris by Vaucanson himself. In 1753 it was acquired by the brothers Pfluger, and then by a person called du Moulin, who exhibited the duck along with two mechanical musicians in St Petersburg. Du Moulin adapted the mechanism so that it became more complicated, thus prohibiting its use by anyone other than himself. The automaton returned from Russia in 1782 and was bought three years later by Beireis, who with some assistance undertook the extremely difficult task of repair and restoration. It was in

Beireis's house at Helmstadt that the automaton was seen by Goethe and his son.

There are no further records of the duck until 1839, when it was discovered in a house in Berlin by the owners of a travelling museum. Their chief clockmaker, Herr Rechsteiner, was given the mammoth task of putting it into order again. By this time there was no part of the bird which did not require extensive repair. Many parts were lost, and most of the mechanism had to be remade. There was a time when Rechsteiner wanted to rebuild the bird embodying new concepts of construction, but the owners insisted upon rebuilding the original Vaucanson duck. The task took three and a half years and cost 6,700 florins. Very soon after the repair was complete, Rechsteiner left his employers and returned to Switzerland in 1844 to make a duck of his own. The owner of the museum, Georges Dietz, showed the duck until it had to be repaired, but by that time Rechsteiner was no longer in his employ and he found that he could not undertake the work himself. The bird was therefore sold to Charles Bontemps in Paris who collected and made singing birds and other automata. He employed his nephew, Seraphin Bontemps, to take the duck all over France.

There is nothing certain known about the fate of Vaucanson's duck after it was acquired by Bontemps. In 1921, however, there was a story being told in Saxony that the bird was still in Germany although no longer in working order. More recently, the curator of the Musée des Arts et Métiers in Paris discovered some photographs of a skeleton automaton duck on a plinth which clearly show the mechanism to be a system of cams and levers turned by weight-driven clockwork. They are supplied with the caption "Pictures of Vaucanson's Duck received from Dresden", and there is no reason to suppose that they are not so. It remains for an ardent collector to rediscover the famous automaton and to bring it back to working order again, but do *not* rely upon the chapter on repairs in this book to tell you how the duck can be restored.

Early History

The story of automata starts many years before the duck of Vaucanson. If we consider that the articulated figure, i.e. one with moving limbs, is a form of automaton then it is possible to trace the beginnings of the art to ancient Egypt, or around 2000 B.C. Several statuettes with articulated arms have been found which date back to that period. The Greeks and Romans also constructed articulated figures, but it was the development of the puppet which made the first major change in the history of automata. It was then possible to exert a greater control over the movement of the limbs and make the mimicry more realistic. The first puppets were perhaps the Wayang figures still used in the shadow theatres of South-east Asia.

Striking Jacks

The automaton as we understand it is an articulated figure which is caused to move by mechanical means. Before clockwork was developed movement could be effected by the use of water, with water wheels and hydrostatic columns, but it was the invention of clockwork which made so many variations possible. Most of the early clockwork driven automata were in fact incorporated into clocks themselves, the figures acting as striking jacks sounding the hours and quarters on bells. The oldest striking jack in the world is in Wells Cathedral where the clock made in 1392 has several automaton figures. The striking jack, "Jack Blandifer," kicks the bells with his heels to strike the quarters, and also sounds the hour by hitting a bell in front of him with a hammer. Moreover, the clock at Wells has an astronomical dial, above which two knights on horseback have a joust at the hour until one is struck off his horse. Other famous "Jacquemart" clocks, the term for those with striking jacks, can be seen at St Mark's Square, Venice, and at Abinger Hammer in Surrey.

Automaton Musicians

The automaton figures on clocks developed until they came to represent musicians and musical groups. While they appeared to play their instruments with realistic movements of the head and fingers, a barrel organ inside the clock would play the music. I shall at this stage return to Vaucanson and the two other figures who appeared alongside the duck; a flute player and a drummer. The drummer played a penny whistle in addition to his drum. Those two automata really were masterpieces of construction, because they actually played the music by blowing air from their lips into the instruments and stopping the keyholes with their fingers. Those who have tried to play a flute will understand how difficult it must have been to construct the figure so that the shape of the mouth and the pressure of air gave a satisfactory tone to the instrument.

Jaquet-Droz

Perhaps the greatest of all the makers of automata was Henry-Louis Jaquet-Droz and his associate Leschot. They developed the ideas of Vaucanson to their full and made two exceptionally fine musical automata. The first was a lady who played the organ. Her whole body moved and the organ was played realistically with the tips of her fingers. Five tunes were played, and during the music the musician's eyes, arms and bosom moved. The organ was a small flute organ similar to those seen in clocks, but was arranged with a keyboard similar to that on a harmonium. Within the musician was set a clockwork driven pin barrel, divided into two halves by a set of large cams which controlled the movement of the arms so that they were in the correct positions over the keyboard. The left- and right-hand sides of the pin barrel were set up with the music for the fingers of the left and right hands. Believe it or not, at the end of each tune a separate mechanism was started which caused the lady to curtsy before going on to the next tune. Henry-Louis Jaquet-Droz and Leschot completed a second automaton musician in 1784 and this time the figure was even more lifelike. As many as

sixteen tunes were played on a harpsichord with the correct pedals being depressed by the foot. Unfortunately this second musician, after many changes of ownership, was sent to St Petersburg, and there is no further record of her. The first can still be seen in the museum at Neuchatel, Switzerland.

Another charming musical automaton can be seen in the Museum of Arts and Crafts in Paris, and this is the dulcimer player of Roentgen and Kintzing, made in 1780. With this figure the mechanism is similar to the Droz-Leschot musician but much simpler. No organ is required and since the dulcimer is struck with only two hammers, there is no mechanism for each separate finger.

The Writer

Pierre, the father of Henry-Louis Jaquet-Droz, made an auto-maton writer and although there are no records as to when it was completed it was in operation before the first musician performed in 1772. The writer is a little boy, just 28 in. tall and made of wood. In his right hand a quill pen is held, while his left arm rests on the desk at which he sits. His head and eyes are in constant motion. When the mechanism is started the boy dips his quill in the ink, shakes it twice and commences to write, starting at the top of the page. The letters are well formed and the quill is removed from the paper between each. Unlike any other automaton writer, he distinguishes between light and heavy strokes of the pen. The sentence is finished with a bold full stop.

The Draughtsman

Pierre Jaquet-Droz's Writer can be seen today in the Neuchatel museum, and beside it and the Musician is the famous Draughtsman of Henry-Louis Jaquet-Droz. This automaton has a simpler mechanism, but produces much more spectacular results. The figure is again a small boy who can draw most delicately four different figures. The head and eyes are moved by levers in the body and the movements to the hand are transmitted from a set of cams through levers in the figure's arm.

These three examples are the finest automata which can still be seen today and are probably as fine as any which have been made. We are fortunate that not all of those wonderful pieces of skill and imagination have been lost like Vaucanson's duck.

Singing Birds in Cages

Apart from the figures he made, Jaquet-Droz was a master of the singing bird. Small singing-bird snuffboxes have already been mentioned in Chapter 5, but far more familiar to most of us today are singing birds in cages. They are still being made today, but it is possible to find some which date back to the mid-nineteeth century. Those made by Jaquet-Droz occasionally appear in the sale room but fetch an extremely high price. The bird is usually in an ornamental cage, gilded and lavishly decorated with flowers and swags. The bottoms of many Jaquet-Droz cages were fitted with a clock so that the face could be seen when the cage was suspended from the ceiling. There were often enamel panels round the sides. The bird sat on a perch with supports at either end and moved its tail, head and beak in time with its song, which was usually in imitation of a nightingale or blackbird. Jaquet-Droz birds often sang a simple tune as well as whistling their bird song.

The modest collector will be much more likely to find the later birds in cages by Bontemps and others. They do not approach the quality of those already mentioned, but are quite pleasing and are great conversation pieces. The later cages are less elaborately decorated and the bird sits on a perch with a single central support which contains the controls for the bird's movements. There are two control wires to the bird, one of which moves the beak and tail together, the other turning the head from side to side. The birdsong is produced in the base of the cage, which contains clockwork to drive a small set of bellows. The air from the bellows is directed to a tiny Swannee whistle, or a whistle whose pitch is altered by sliding a piston in and out of it. The position of the piston and hence the note is controlled by a cam on the clockwork which also controls

a valve to shut off the air, giving a cheeping sound. It is possible to have more than one bird at a time in the cage and in such cases each bird can be recognised by its own song.

Most of the better quality birdcages were made in Switzerland or France between 1820 and 1880, but after this date the quality dropped and many were made in Germany. The later German birds are smaller and not so ornate. The sides of the cage bottom are often made of metal instead of carved and gilded wood and the bird is often a small humming bird. The song, however, is pleasing and is certainly good enough for your collection if the mechanism is adjusted well.

Monkeys and Musicians

Monkeys and musicians always succeeded in fascinating the automaton-maker. It is possible to see in a monkey all the human weaknesses without actually identifying any of them with yourself. We laugh loudest at a monkey scratching itself when we have an itch which we cannot reach. Musicians also are ideal for imitation for they not only have distinctive movements which can be copied, but also the music itself can be represented with a musical box in the base of the automaton.

In Vienna towards the middle of the last century a series of fine automata were made which use both monkeys and musicians. There were of course several combinations, but often the automaton was a musical duet playing for a dancing monkey. Dressed in contemporary costumes, a pianist and a fiddler played their instruments realistically while a small monkey, also dressed, danced up and down between them. The three would be set on a base measuring about 10 in. by 5 in. and about 2 in. high. In this base was a small musical movement by one of the famous Austrian or Czechoslovakian makers such as Olbrich of Vienna or Rzebitschek from Prague. Such movements, compared with those of Swiss make, are usually of superb quality, the music being set up with the utmost precision. Two tunes are usually found, often a waltz and a march.

91

These Viennese automata are rare and are often in an extreme state of disrepair when they are found. They are of such fine quality, however, that they are well worth the work of restoration.

Towards the end of the nineteenth century a large number of good quality automata were made by a maker who put his initials "LB" on the key. It is not certainly known who this was, but popular belief supposes that it was Lucienne Bontemps, a member of the family who at one time owned Vaucanson's duck. Bontemps automata are often to be seen for sale although they are usually fairly expensive. The figures of humans or monkeys are about 18 in. high on a square base which contains the musical movement and mechanism. A popular type is the "Smoker". This automaton can be either a man or a monkey and has a cigarette holder in the right hand. When a lighted cigarette is put into the holder and the mechanism started, the automaton raises the cigarette to his mouth, rolls his eyes as he takes a puff, lowers the cigarette again, and then puffs out a cloud of smoke. In fact a tube in the arm of the model takes the smoke from the cigarette, and blows it out through the figure's mouth by means of a small set of bellows.

Another charming model is that of a pretty young lady who is seated at her dressing-table. While she admires herself in front of the mirror, she either brushes her hair or pours perfume onto a handkerchief which is applied to her face.

Magicians and Acrobats

The illusionist and conjuror was a popular man of entertainment at the end of the nineteenth century and so many imitative automata were made. The commonest of these is the trick with the two cups. The magician sits at a table on which there are two upturned cups. The cups are lifted up one by one to expose ever-changing articles beneath them. A dice, a ball and a mouse are often used. A musical box in the base plays while the magician performs his trick.

Acrobatic automata are ideal for showing the skill of the auto-maton-maker. A famous acrobat by Decamps can be seen in Paris.

The figure rests on a plinth and as the mechanism is started he raises himself into a handstand, finally separating his feet to do the splits. A similar feat is also performed by other automata using the back of a chair on which to balance.

Mechanical Pictures

One day you'll meet someone who will tell you, "I saw the most extraordinary thing today—a mechanical picture, and the owner tells me that it was the only one ever made! There is a ship on a rough sea, pitching and tossing in the waves, while over a bridge across the water there is a squad of soldiers marching towards a windmill with revolving sails. In the distance, a balloon ascends and floats away. All this is to the accompaniment of music from a musical box." There will follow some extremely complicated directions as to how the picture can be found and the footnote that it is a family heirloom and under no circumstances for sale. Be that as it may, it is always worth the trouble of following up such directions to see the mechanical picture described to you.

A great number of these mechanical pictures and landscapes were made, and some of them date back to 1750. By 1850, however, they were made in great numbers to a more or less standard pattern and were not of fine quality. Most collectors will agree that what they desire most is something of which only one has been made. The early mechanical pictures come into this category. They were often extremely complicated as can be understood from the following description, taken from *Automata*, by Chapuis and Droz, of a mechanical picture made in 1759 and now to be seen in Paris:

"The picture has a gilt frame and gilt scrolls in the corners. It is very interesting, particularly for the variety of scenes which it shows and the large number of animated figures and objects in it. In the background stands a castle surrounded by fine parks. On the right, at a chosen moment, some dogs jump up, chase each other, and disappear behind the buildings. On the left two people are playing with a ball on the lawn. Further forward are some gardens where

two marquises pay their respects to a great lady, and in return she bows to them. On the road in front of the castle grounds a number of people pass—a wagoner driving his cart with slatted sides, some sheep, a peasant woman and her cow, a small wagon etc. Further forward flows a river where two workmen are busy floating timber and where there are rowing boats laden with people. These, like the people passing along the road, are animated and make various movements as they pass across the picture. In the foreground on the left stand two laundresses working with all their might, and on the right a fisherman casts and draws in his line, while next to him is a woman and her child who wave their hands. This piece belongs to Madame de Pompadour whose arms it bears, and shows her chateau of Saint-Ouen."

Such a picture is vastly superior to those made a hundred years later, and it is very unlikely that you will ever be offered one. But it is part of the thrill of collecting when you know that the chance of owning such a piece is always there, however remote. If you do find an early and complicated picture like the one just described, and it is offered to you, accept the offer, even if the picture is broken. With ingenuity and patience it can usually be restored, and such an eighteenth-century picture will be an extremely rare piece when it is working again.

Later pictures, made in about 1900, had no music and the moving parts were made of thin card. Comical scenes were depicted and usually only the eyes, mouth and limbs of the figures were capable of movement. One such picture is of a man trying to hit a mouse with a fly swat. The weapon is raised several times slowly in order to take aim as the mouse cautiously emerges from a hole in the wall. The man then strikes hard at the mouse which nips smartly back into the hole; the man's jaw drops in dismay and his eyes close. Cats became popular at this time for some reason, and it is not unusual to find a picture which shows a musical quartet of moving cats.

Rabbits are usually seen coming out of hats, but in the world of automata, the mechanical rabbit prefers to appear out of a lettuce. When the lettuce is wound up and switched on, the leaves near the top separate slowly to the accompaniment of music, and the head of a rabbit appears. As the rabbit raises his head he sniffs cautiously around and shakes his ears. Then suddenly, something startles him and he retreats, and the lettuce shuts with a bang. A collector has a good chance of finding a rabbit in a lettuce. They were made during this century up to about 1925.

Mechanical lions were also made recently. The beast is wound and then released. After swaying backwards and forwards on its hind legs once or twice, the lion finds its balance and springs forwards with a wild roar. Fortunately for the timid such automata are rare.

Automata cannot be discussed without mention being made of the silver swan. This is perhaps the most important mechanical animal to be seen in this country. Now on display at the Bowes Museum, Barnard Castle, Co. Durham, this magnificent bird, made of silver, floats in a stream of twisted glass rods from which it takes small fish with its beak. The neck of the bird is made up of rings of silver which are put together in such a way that the most realistic swan-like movements are possible. As the swan dips its beak in the stream, a tiny silver fish appears in the beak and is then swallowed. The mechanism is most complicated and extremely powerful, having to drive not only the swan's neck but also the many twisted glass rods which simulate the stream. There is also a twelve-bell six-air musical carillon which accompanies the swan's action. Unfortunately, the automaton has recently been fitted with a penny-in-the-slot device which allows it to be used far too frequently for a machine so old and delicate. The maker is not known with certainty, but it is thought that the swan was made prior to 1774 when it is recorded as being in the museum of James Cox the Clockmaker. It is a great pity that such a masterpiece cannot be attributed to a maker, but the only names which appear on the swan are those of repairers who scratched their names on the

silver from time to time. There is a theory however, that the swan could be the work of Vaucanson, who was known to be very interested in chain drive for the control of his automata. The neck of the swan is actuated in this way and so could have been made by Vaucanson or one of his pupils.

Above, eight-air lever-wind music box by Ducommun-Girod, *c.* 1870; *below*, lever-wind box with zither attachment by L. A. Grosclaude of Geneva, *c.* 1880

Interior of six-air organo-piccolo box by Nicole Frères, No. 46649, *c.* 1885. The engine-turning can be seen on the brasswork; *below*, exterior of the same box. The case is inlaid with pewter banding

8

Buying and Repairing a Musical Box

When you start collecting musical boxes you will be in urgent need of help and expert advice when it comes to buying a box in doubtful condition. The inexperienced collector tends to view the world through rose-coloured spectacles, especially when he sees a rare box, so when offered a box in imperfect condition, you should be objectively critical and not carried away by the collector's urge. This feeling serves you best when you are actually looking for a box but can lead you sadly astray when it has been found.

The reasons for buying a box can be many. Perhaps you are looking for a type so far absent from your collection, or it could be that you are making a collection all of one type. For example, I spent a long time finding my first mandolin box, and having found it liked it so much that I have since acquired several more. Some collect boxes so that they have a representation of every period of manufacture. Collecting in this way leads to a study of the development and history of both music boxes and also the popular music of the time. There are some who buy for investment, and here music boxes are to be recommended. An increase in value of 25 per cent per annum is predicted at the present time. It is always good to know that you can get your money back at any time on a fairly expensive purchase. Incidentally it must be remembered that the better the condition of the music box, the quicker its value is likely to rise. A box in poor or unoriginal condition is always of doubtful value.

It may be that you wish to buy a music box as a gift for someone who is not a collector. In such a case, you should buy a box in good mechanical condition, which is unlikely to require attention in the foreseeable future. If good music is required, choose one which is well set up with music of quality, and if they like furniture, choose a box in a pretty case. As the recipient is not a collector the name of Nicole Frères will mean less to him than well-arranged Gilbert and Sullivan in a finely inlaid rosewood case.

Condition at Time of Purchase

I have analysed the motives involved in the purchase of a music box and shall now pass to the assessment of its condition. The first and most obvious feature is the case and a lot can be told from its appearance. If care has been taken of the case, leaving it clean and polished with the veneer still intact, there is a good chance that the movement has also been treated with care. If the wood is warped and the veneer lifting, the damp which caused such damage will almost certainly have affected the movement. Dents and scratches could have been caused by children and if the case has been marked in this way you can be sure that the movement also will have been maltreated.

Having got a first impression from the state of the case, open the lid and examine the works. Do not be misled by first appearances. Often when the works are dirty and dusty it implies that they are in their original condition and have not been tampered with at any time. Such a box, although looking as though it has never been cleaned or cared for, is a good find.

If the comb is damaged with broken teeth or tips of teeth, the box has probably had a "run" and you should at once look for all the other signs. The cylinder pins will be bent or broken and there is usually deep scoring to be seen at the base end of the cylinder where the resonators have been lifted onto it. A box in this condition can be repaired but the repairs will be costly, so you should not pay much for it in the first place. Only the best boxes are worth the trouble and cost of repinning.

If you find that a box has had a run never try to wind it up. This will only cause it to run again and increase the damage. Turn the cylinder gently by hand and the fault in the mechanism should show itself.

Sometimes you will find a box that has been played so frequently that it is literally worn out. The teeth are worn and the cylinder pins bent and broken, but with careful attention this box can be restored. Worn comb teeth can be realigned by honing them on a piece of fine emery paper stuck to a sheet of glass, and a limited number of cylinder pins can be straightened. If very many pins are out of true then the cylinder should be repinned. At present there is no service in this country for repinning cylinders, although a few individuals have undertaken this extremely tedious task on one or two of our boxes. A company in Switzerland will repin a cylinder for a very modest cost—about £20 for a 13 in. Nicole Frères cylinder—but it will take about a year before you get the cylinder back. £20 may seem a lot of money, but it represents about 20 hours work and could increase the value of your box by as much as £100.

If buying a damaged box, ask yourself whether it is a viable proposition to carry out the necessary repairs. This depends on the box. If it is rare then you would be justified in spending the time and money on it, but if the box is of poor quality think twice before spending more than the value of the box on repairs to it. Having decided to buy, then all your efforts should be spent in seeing that the necessary work is carried out correctly. Great damage can be done, and often is done, by careless handling on the part of the inexpert repairer. If you decide to do some work on the box yourself, I suggest you consult Graham Webb's book *The Cylinder Musical Box Handbook.*

Dismantling a Movement

If you do not know the correct procedure of dismantling and cleaning a movement, then it is better to hand the box to someone

who does, rather than make a mistake and finish with a box in worse condition than when you first found it. There is a strict order of dismantling which should always be used. The sequence is as follows:

Remove the movement from the case.
Remove the comb.
Let the spring down.
Remove the wheel train.
Remove the tune changer.
Remove the cylinder.
Remove the spring barrel assembly.
Remove the control levers from under the bedplate.

At this stage there is a danger of having a jumble of loose parts and screws, and by the time you have cleaned them all, you may well have forgotten where they belong. To avoid this a large cardboard box should be prepared with holes in the top, so that the screws can be placed in the holes as they are removed. If the holes are arranged in the same relative positions as the screws on the movement, there will be no danger of forgetting which screw is which. On the earlier movements this is of great importance, since each screw is individually threaded for its own hole and there is virtually no interchangeability. Sometimes the comb screws are marked with dots to give their correct sequence. A screw out of place could affect the comb register.

The comb can easily be damaged when it is removed from the bedplate. Great care must therefore be taken. First remove the comb screws and put them in correct order in the holes on the cardboard box. The comb must now be removed without letting it move forward against the cylinder. If this happens, the dampers will be bent and teeth may be broken. Put a small centre punch in one of the screw holes and, as the back of the comb is eased up with a screwdriver, pull the centre punch to the rear. The comb will lift off quite easily without touching the cylinder. Do not remove the comb one

end at a time. Unless it is lifted off evenly, a broken tooth can be the result. After removal the comb is very vulnerable, so it should be wrapped in a sheet of newspaper and put away carefully until it is required.

To let the tension off the spring it is possible to allow the movement to run down normally, but this takes time and is not possible if the wheel train is jammed for some reason. The alternative is to let the spring down manually. To do this, take up the tension on the key or lever and then release the retaining pawl. Holding the key firmly, let it turn and then return the pawl at convenient intervals. Continue until there is no tension left in the spring. A box with the spring wound must be considered capable of causing damage to itself, so always let the spring down if you are about to undertake work on the wheel train.

The wheel train and tune changer are removed without any special problems, and this will leave you with the cylinder. This, like the comb, is prone to damage and because it carries the musical score controls the quality of the box. After the cylinder bridges have been unscrewed, lift the cylinder off the bedplate with care. As with the comb it is best to wrap the cylinder in a sheet of newspaper until you are ready to clean it. Above all, do not place it on a hard surface or put it down where it can roll about. There should be no special problems in the removal of the spring barrel assembly.

Repairs

We shall consider only that work which can be carried out without great problems to the different parts of the music box. It is most important when buying to know what can and cannot be done in the way of repairs. Many times have I been told that new combs can be made, when being given a hard sell on a box with a damaged comb. This is not true. At present combs cannot be made economically for old boxes, so a box with a very badly damaged comb can only be considered for spare parts. A damaged box is only a good proposition if it can be repaired.

101

The Case

There is really nothing which cannot be carried out in the way of repairs to the case if you know a good cabinet maker. Woodworm can be killed with any good proprietary fluid and the holes filled with plastic wood, which is then coloured so that it does not show. If the worm has attacked a large area just under the surface the damage is sometimes so bad that the wood has become soft and spongy. When this has happened the panel should be partly or completely replaced.

The lids of many boxes are decorated with veneer in the form of a marquetry design which is often missing a few pieces. These can be matched and replaced, once the correct colour of wood has been found. Various veneers can be purchased in the Shoreditch area of London, or any other area where there is a concentration of cabinet making. The following woods were often used: rosewood, satinwood, boxwood, green sycamore, burr walnut, burr oak, boxwood stringing and tulipwood banding. Oak, mahogany and walnut veneer were usually not used, but the sides of the case were often made of solid walnut veneered with rosewood. The bottom of the box is best made of deal, which has a broad grain and acts as a good sounding board.

When the cases were originally made, they were assembled with the aid of a good cabinet maker's glue, and repairs should be carried out using a similar adhesive. Croid Aero glue or Seccotine will do very well but I do not recommend that you use cellulose or rubber adhesives, since their appearance will detract from the originality of the case. A good P.V.A. resin glue can also be used for sticking woodwork.

After repairing the case, finish it in a fashion which suits its age. Earlier unveneered cases would almost certainly have been waxed originally, and it is quite easy to clean and wax such a box when you are fortunate enough to find one. The later cases were usually french polished and it is quite in order to finish your collection in this way. If you ask a polisher how it can be done, he will tell you that it will

take a lifetime to learn and there is no quick way to success. I suspect that this stems from the age-old habit of protecting your profession by keeping the tricks of the trade secret. With a little practice and patience you will find that you can attain quite an adequate finish. Surface preparation is the secret. If the surface is smooth and flat and well sealed very few coats of polish have to be applied to give a good shine. Sealing lacquers such as Duraxcote are easily bought and should be applied by brush. This sealer is allowed to dry thoroughly and sanded smooth, finishing with flour grade paper. Coats of french polish should then be applied with a cloth pad. Sand down between coats, apply coats thinly and concentrate on the edges of the panel. The final shine can be obtained by wiping off with a cotton wool pad soaked in a very small amount of methylated spirit, but it is easier to leave the polish for a day or two and then rub down vigorously with a cotton wool pad soaked in french polish reviver. The golden rule of the french polisher is that he is never in a hurry.

The Comb

The comb of the music box is the musical instrument and should therefore be treated with the greatest care. The tuning of the teeth is critical and can easily be spoiled by incorrect cleaning. Whenever a comb is cleaned remove the dirt but never the metal of the comb itself. Non-abrasive substances are the order of the day. Start cleaning with solvents and brushes, and if the dirt is heavy use a stiffer brush. Rust can be scraped away with the edge of a razor blade and the spot cleaned with a glass fibre stick, but you should avoid the use of emery paper and never polish or burnish the comb as this could seriously affect the tuning. Always treat with suspicion a comb which has been burnished or polished. Extensive retuning could be required.

Dampers can be replaced with the correct damper wire but they must be fixed with taper pins of the correct size, or the teeth will go

out of tune. If you use the original pins there will be no fear of detuning the comb.

Very often you will find that one or more of the teeth has broken off. Occasionally this has been caused by careless handling—such as dropping the key on to the comb—but usually the teeth have been broken because the box has had a run. It is a fairly easy matter to replace one or two broken teeth, but if many are missing replacement and subsequent tuning will be difficult, especially if the teeth are close together. The repair will also be hard to conceal.

In order to replace a broken tooth, good tools, a little skill and a lot of patience are needed. The method most usually employed is to file a notch in the comb behind the missing tooth and slightly wider than the tooth. A tooth the right size and pitch is then cut from a length of spare comb and the heel of it is filed up so that it fits exactly into the notch in the comb. Since the fit is all important to the eventual tone of the tooth, good files and careful work are essential. The tooth is fixed into the comb with ordinary solder, but it is sometimes difficult to get the solder to run into the joint. This is because the large bulk of the comb is taking the heat away too quickly. Heat the comb up in boiling water first and you will find that it requires very little extra heat from the iron to melt the solder. After soldering, the new tooth is trimmed to match the rest of the comb and then tuned. To raise the pitch you must remove metal from the end of the tooth with a file, and to lower the pitch make the end slightly heavier with a small blob of solder.

Very often only the tip of the tooth has been broken. A tip can be replaced by cutting a thin slot into the tooth and then soldering a new tip onto it. The slot should be at least $\frac{1}{4}$ in. long, and the new part can be fashioned out of steel of the grade from which magazine staples are made. In fact, staples hammered to fit into the notch do very well, being soft enough to solder and file and also stiff enough to play the tooth. The new tip is trimmed and tuned after fitting.

The Wheel Train

There is no damage to the wheel train which cannot be repaired. But if it has suffered, do look for all the other things that go with it, such as damage to the comb and cylinder. A stripped endless screw or first wheel could be the reason why it is not running properly, and replacement parts for these can be obtained by any of the well-known music box dealers. If the jewel end stone is missing you should get a replacement. Ask any jewel house in Clerkenwell for a garnet, cut flat on the bottom. If you have difficulty in finding a garnet the right size a good temporary measure is to insert a strip of stainless razor blade under the endstone plate. It is very hard and provides a good bearing surface. The wheel train will not run properly if the bearings are so worn that they are oval and not round. They should then be rebushed and this is quite a simple task for any clockmaker.

Sometimes, try how you will, the wheel train just will not run, however well the depth of the endless screw is adjusted. Usually it has to be run in if some of the parts are new and it can be extremely difficult to get it started. I recommend that you try a little Rocol 120 watchmakers' black oil on the endless screw in such a case. This is a lubricant which contains molybdenum and gives the working surfaces a very slippery and extremely thin layer. A fault of the wheel train which can pass unnoticed is a flat top to the endless screw. It should be domed to spin correctly on the endstone, and a flat one can very quickly be returned to its original domed shape by turning it in a lathe against an Arkansas stone or barber's hone.

The Cylinder

The cylinder carries the musical score of the music box and so its importance cannot be over-emphasised. Before buying always inspect the cylinder with the greatest care, looking for bent and broken pins or other signs of rough treatment. Every pin which is out of place or missing is a note lost. Sometimes it is possible to bend the pins back so that they are straight again, but this is only

practicable when a few are affected. When the number of bent pins is very large, restoration is difficult if not impossible. You will find it very hard to bend the pins back to the required angle, but if you use a hypodermic needle with the end cut off, you will find its length will clearly show the correct angle to which the pins have to be returned.

Widespread damage to the cylinder can only be repaired by completely repinning it. There is no way of partly repinning a cylinder, it is a case of all or nothing. The wax is removed from within the cylinder by melting it and then the pins are dissolved in dilute sulphuric acid, which leaves the brass intact as long as it is not left in the acid for too long. Three or four days is usually long enough to remove the pins completely. The cylinder is washed out, first with a solution of ammonia and then with fresh water. The pins must now be replaced. Originally, sticks of pin wire were obtainable, and these were nicked every $\frac{1}{4}$ in. or so. They could be inserted into the holes and broken off at the nicks. Today the wire comes in coils and is inserted into the holes in the cylinder with a special tool, which inserts the wire and cuts it off more or less in one movement. Speed is essential since to repin a normal cylinder at least 3,000 pins will be required. If you are working at the rate of three a minute it will take you about $16\frac{1}{2}$ hours just to put in the pins. A large Grande Format Overture Box will have about 50,000 pins in the cylinder, but in spite of this staggering number they are still being repinned in Switzerland by Baud Frères L'Auberson at Ste Croix. The cost makes it very worth while for any box of good quality.

After all the pins have been inserted, the wax is heated and poured back into the cylinder. The cylinder is spun while the wax cools, finally the new pins are "shaved" on a lathe so that they are all exactly the same length.

Very occasionally you will find a box which has been kept in a place which is too hot, causing the wax to move and distort the cylinder. This distortion is not usually visible but shows itself as a

change in volume of the music as the pins move closer and further away from the comb. If the distortion is small the cylinder can be made true by skimming the pins in a lathe, but often the fault is so great that it cannot be corrected. Such a box cannot usually be repaired.

To clean a cylinder use a shoe brush with long bristles. Take care not to allow the wooden handle to graze against the pins. Clean first with a metal polish such as Brasso and then finish with a silver plate powder in methylated spirit. Polish the powder off with a clean dry brush. After cleaning the cylinder check that the holes in the end are completely free of both wax and polish, and that the cylinder moves freely up and down the spindle.

The Spring Barrel Assembly

As with the wheel train there is no damage to this part which cannot be repaired. Wheels can be cut and springs replaced without difficulty. Beware, however of removing the spring of a music box yourself. It is large and extremely strong. A bad injury could be caused by allowing the spring to slip when it is half in and half out of the spring barrel. When you do decide to take the spring out, put the spring barrel firmly in a vice and remove the spring coil by coil wearing thick gardening gloves. Above all, if you feel the spring begin to slip in your hands, hold on! The new spring should be lubricated with a good molybdenum sulphide grease.

Reassembly and Adjustment

Having restored the individual parts of your box to the best condition that you can, it remains to assemble them so that the box plays well. Even if the box was a good player when you bought it, the process of cleaning will have affected the speed, register and dampers, and even the resonance of the movement in the case will have been altered. Often the result can be disappointing to the extent that you may wonder whether it was wise to have cleaned the movement at all. Well it *was* wise, because you have stopped the processes of corrosion by removing rust and damp; you have

107

stopped the processes of wear by removing the dirt and renewing the oil, and you have reduced the risk of a run by replacing worn parts in the wheel train.

The movement must now be adjusted. Start with the comb off and check that the clockwork runs freely and at the right speed. Adjusting the fan on the endless screw alters the speed. Move the vanes out to slow down and vice versa. Next check that the tune changer is working correctly, and that the cylinder moves back freely to the bottom of the snail when it should. If you have left some polish under the snail it will make it hard to turn and may stop the movement. Does the stop work function properly? The stop lever should snap into its recess in the great wheel and trip the stop bar on the endless screw at the same time. The stop bar should be firm on the endless screw so that the fan cannot revolve when the stop lever is up. If a few turns are made after the lever comes up, the lever can be strained and bent where it bears on the great wheel.

Not until you are happy that the clockwork of the movement functions properly should you start to think about the music. When you are satisfied, let the cylinder revolve until it is at the step at the bottom of the snail or in the position for tune No. 1, and allow it to stop. Put the comb on carefully and screw it in place with two or three screws. Check the register by looking at the tips of the teeth. They should point exactly at the register lines on the cylinder. After cleaning, some adjustment may be necessary to the register screw at the end of the cylinder to bring them back in line.

Adjusting the Comb

Now try the music. Often the comb will be adjusted so that it is too near or too far from the cylinder. The music should be clear and bright but the teeth should not be lifted more than about $\frac{1}{10}$ in. or so. If they are being lifted too far, the comb is too near the cylinder. This can be corrected by either packing the front edge of the comb with a thin strip of paper, or screwing in the comb setting screw slightly. When the teeth are lifted too little and the music is too

soft, you can bring the comb nearer to the cylinder by gently tapping the back of it with a wooden hammer until the volume is correct. If the comb is a long one, care has to be taken to adjust the ends relative to one another. If the treble end of the comb is too near to the cylinder box it will play arpeggios when you should be getting chords. When the comb is correctly adjusted put all the screws in their correct holes and screw up tight.

The damper wires always need adjustment after cleaning. They should be carefully reshaped and replaced where necessary to eliminate the squeaks and groans.

Finally the movement is returned to the case and screwed in. Make sure that the feet on the bedplate touch the bottom of the case and that the sides fit round the movement snugly. Packing pieces are often necessary to ensure this. If contact with the bottom and sides is not good the music will not sound as it should.

Curing Vibrations

Having got to this stage, you will almost certainly hear a multitude of rattles. They can easily be cured once they have been found, but it is not always an easy job finding them. The case lock is the prime offender, and since it is seldom used, can be filled with glue or plastic wood. It is hard to find a lock which works and does not rattle. A loose inner glass lid is often the source of a rattle, and it can be secured by forcing an adhesive under the putty. The control levers under the bedplate were always wrapped with a turn or two of string before they were screwed on, so make sure that the string has been put back after you clean them and before they are returned to the movement. They are very prone to vibration. If the stop works rattle it can usually be cured by setting the return spring slightly tighter, and the same can apply to the winding lever.

Eventually, after very many hours, you will have a box which plays as well as it did when it was new, and you will have the pleasure of knowing that you recognised it for what it could be restored to, and that all the hours you have put into it were worth the effort.

Repairs to a Disc Music Box

I have so far concentrated on cylinder boxes, and although much of what has been said can be applied to disc boxes, there are some features associated with them which require special attention. All repairs to the case and clockwork are similar, no matter what the machine is, and the disc machine comb is in many ways similar to that on the cylinder box. You will remember, however, that the disc box comb does not have dampers pinned into the teeth and is played with star wheels. Although this is a much simpler arrangement, the star wheels cause much more wear to the comb than a cylinder would have done. Quite deep grooves are formed which must be ground out by honing the comb on a sheet of emery paper stuck to a flat sheet of glass.

To clean a disc music box, the works are first removed from the case and then the motor assembly is taken off. This leaves a bedplate with the combs and star wheel assembly on it. The combs are removed easily, but it is unwise to remove the star wheel assembly unless it is broken or in a very bad condition. It is very accurately set up and the slightest alteration of its position relative to the combs would affect the music. After the damper bars have been removed, clean the star wheels with a stiff brush and spirit. They are in contact with the disc while it plays, collecting a great deal of dirt between them, and are often jammed with projections broken from the disc. Broken projections must be most carefully removed because a star wheel that does not revolve freely will only damage other discs. A star wheel point which is burred or bent over will also cause jamming, so it must be filed or bent back to shape again to cure the fault.

Care of Discs

The musical programme of a disc machine is of course the disc itself, and because they are replaceable—not easily mind you—the collector tends to treat them with less care than the cylinder of his cylinder box. A disc which has been allowed to grow rusty will

deposit rust in the star wheel assembly which will in turn damage other discs. Discs are best stored in a dry room, either hung up or between sheets of cardboard in a box. If they are kept side by side without anything between them, try to arrange them so that they are front-to-front and back-to-back. Stored this way they will either slide harmlessly against one another or key together with the projections making movement impossible. If a disc's projections are placed against the front of a neighbouring disc the two will slide together, breaking and bending projections. Always insert pieces of board.

After assembly, the disc box must be adjusted. First ensure that the star wheels are playing the combs correctly by rotating them manually, then put on a disc. You may find that an adjustment to the centre spindle in height and position is necessary to get the disc to play in register.

When projections are broken off a disc, it is possible to replace them. For a steel disc new projections are formed from steel of the right thickness and soldered into position. If the disc is made of zinc, ordinary solder will not take, but you can use an epoxy resin adhesive such as Araldite. This will give a good bond which is quite adequate for the job.

Final Advice

You must have gathered from this chapter that a collector's day is never done unless he is lucky enough to find a box which requires no work or restoration. So do try to assess what has to be done to a box before committing yourself to buying it. The following advice could be helpful:

(a) If the box is in playing order, make sure all the tunes play properly.

(b) If the box is not in playing order, inspect the comb and cylinder carefully for damage.

(c) If the music is poor, decide whether it can be restored without repinning.

(d) If repinning is necessary, decide whether the box is worth such an expense. A rare box is nearly always worth it unless too many teeth are broken.

(e) Do not try to restore to perfection a box which was never of good quality.

For those who admire fine cabinet work you notice that no mention is made of the case. But unless the case is literally falling apart from worm, there is really nothing which cannot be restored.

A final word of advice: if you can't do it properly yourself, put the job of restoration into the hands of someone who can. A large number of musical boxes were made but few survive, and a job done badly on one of them will mean one survivor less. A run caused by a careless amateur can cost £200 in about 5 seconds.

Symphonion in moulded and veneered case, *c.* 1895; *below*, animated picture driven by clockwork, *c.* 1880. The mouse always manages to escape

Above, *left*, miniature street barrel piano by Henry Distin who was apprenticed to Joseph Hicks in 1850; *right*, the 'Seraphone' paper roll reed organette, *c.* 1885; *below*, good quality ten-air drum-and-bell box by Nicole Frères, No. 50389, *c.* 1890

9

The Industry Today

It is more than a hundred and seventy years since the music box was invented, and as you have seen there have been very many influences on its development since 1796. This development was slow initially, and it was not until 1815 that the industry first became organised on a company basis. The techniques of manufacture had become good enough by 1840 to start producing music boxes of special design with two or more combs, or with mandolin combs; and by 1860 or so, manufacturers had begun to think about mass production. By about 1870 the downhill path had begun; the slope was gentle at first, but the factory technology could not keep pace with the rapid increase in rate of production and cuts were made which inevitably lowered the quality of the music boxes. The competition between companies first made them try to make boxes on a more grandiose scale than their rivals, but as nearly always happens, price became the most important factor in the end.

It was in 1890 that the first serious challenge was made to the cylinder music box by disc machines. Unlike the cylinder musical box industry, the manufacture of the disc machine developed exceedingly rapidly and vast quantities were produced over a period of only twenty-five years, when in 1914 the industry in Europe was killed by the Great War. Although the first phonograph recording had been made by Thomas Edison in 1877, it was the need for accurate reproduction during the war which really helped the phonograph to develop, and by the end of the war in 1918, the capabilities of the gramophone were so good that there was virtually no need for any form of mechanical music.

The period between the two great world wars was one of rapid technological development and of political and sociological uncertainty. A great number of the Victorian music boxes had been bought by the British, who were one of the richest nations in the world during her reign. In 1920, however, music boxes were old hat, and although we were a country of great prosperity we were spending our money on motor-cars and wireless sets instead. The Swiss makers had lost their original market and many of them returned to making watches, which now tell us whether we have missed our flight or not. Le Coultre & Cie., founded in 1833, are now making some of the finest watches in the world under the trade mark Jaeger-le-Coultre at Le Sentier, a small village at the sound end of the Lac de Joux. The Paillard family are based at Ste Croix where they make Paillard-Bolex ciné cameras and projectors and the Hermes typewriter. They started to make phonographs when the music box market was finished but their production did not last long. Audemars-Piguet & Cie., two important musical box names, combined in 1875 to found one of the top watchmaking firms in the world at Bern. There is a company at La Chaux de Fonds, Fils de George Ducommun, who make watch cases and may well be descended from Ducommun Girod. Also at La Chaux de Fonds, Marcel Dubois S.A. makes scientific and industrial instruments and watches. There was a famous musical watchmaker in the same town in 1820.

Ste Croix

The centre of the modern musical box industry built up round the two towns of Ste Croix and L'Auberson, which are only four kilometres from one another in the mountains twenty kilometres north-west of the southern tip of the Lac de Neuchatel. Today there are nine registered companies who make, repair and market musical boxes and movements in the two towns. It seems that the industry is again on the increase and that the movements are improving in quality and growing in size. For a long time the only

musical movements made were very small and designed to be put into jewel cases, cigarette boxes or other items whose saleability could be improved by the novelty of including music. The movements are designed so that they can be mass-produced and the size of the comb—up to 18 teeth—restricts the quality of music which can be attempted. However, although they do not compare with the antique music box, they make splendid souvenirs and can be a good way of collecting national melodies. I have a modern plastic bell amongst the antiques in my collection, which plays *Berliner Luft* simply but well. It serves to remind me of a very pleasant visit to that city. The musical movement in the bell is made by a firm called Lador S.A., founded in 1825, who make musical movements in Ste Croix. The comb of the movement has 19 teeth and the cylinder is diecast complete with projections instead of being pinned. Studs on the great wheel revolve a colour slide holder so that views of Berlin can be seen as the music plays.

Also manufacturing in Ste Croix we have Breitler S.A. founded in 1929, Les Fils de John Jaccard founded in 1862 by Jules Jaccard, and finally Reuge S.A. who are one of the most important modern manufacturers. It was in 1880 that Charles Reuge, whose family had previously specialised in watchmaking, undertook the manufacture of a series of watches with musical movements intended for export, in particular to the Far East. The company then grew from strength to strength, and in the space of seventy-five years passed from a simple workshop to a semi-industrial business, eventually to become a large modern factory. The industrialisation of the craft posed great problems, but Reuge has tried to mould together the two forms of industry by combining the old techniques and traditions with an economic production programme. The cylinders they make are pinned in the normal way and their combs have between 18 and 72 teeth. These larger movements really are superb in quality and the music approaches the standards reached by the old masters. The cylinders are fitted with a tune changer and anything between two and six airs can be played. I recently heard one of their boxes play

the overture to *The Thieving Magpie* in three parts, and though the playing time was not as great as that offered by the old thick cylinders, the quality of the music and its setting was excellent. Reuge also make a series of automata which are very similar in character to those made during the latter half of the last century. A magician, a guitarist and a harpsichord player are all represented. They also make singing birds in cages which are very similar to those made by Charles Bontemps, including a cage containing three birds which sing independently.

L'Auberson

Just four kilometres up the road from Ste Croix is the tiny village of L'Auberson, which holds no less than five registered musical box makers. Thorens S.A., founded in 1883, now use the name Melodies S.A. and still make large quantities of music boxes of all types. The firm John & Edward Cuendet, founded in 1895, still exists and movements by them are to be found in many toys and novelties. Often their cylinders are not pinned, but have projections raised from the metal of the cylinder itself. Another firm of long standing is André Gueissaz & Cie., which was founded in 1849. There is a recent company in L'Auberson called Frank Margot, which specialises in manivelles or hand operated music boxes.

Perhaps the most important L'Auberson company to the collector is that of Baud Frères, under the Direction of Monsieur Frédéric Baud. He is the man who will repin the cylinder of an antique musical box should it be required. This company with a small but very highly skilled staff has managed to preserve all the finer points of craftsmanship relating to the repair of music boxes. Not only will they repin cylinders, but I have seen extraordinarily fine repairs to broken combs, with new teeth inserted so that the repair can barely be seen. You might think that it would be too uncertain to depend upon repairs alone, but the firm has almost more work than it has time to complete and there is a long waiting list of boxes to be treated.

Japan

As with many other industries, Japan has entered on the scene, and is now producing great quantities of musical boxes and musical movements which are competing with those made in Switzerland. They are all small movements of good quality, but the Japanese do not seem to have achieved anything which has not been done already in Switzerland, except perhaps at times to make more of a lower priced product. There are seven main manufacturers of movements in Japan, including Tokyo Pigeon Orugoru Co. Ltd., Tokyo Seiki Orgel Co. Ltd., and Sankyo Sieki Mfg. Co. Ltd. of Nagano. It seems a pity that the Japanese have not developed some new ideas based on their introduction to the Swiss industry. Perhaps the Swiss, renowned as perfectionists, developed the music box about as far as will ever be possible.

The Future

Time and time again we find that some form of mechanical operation has been replaced by an electronic system. Edison's phonograph produced sound when a diaphragm was vibrated mechanically by the action of the stylus on the "hills" and "dales" of the cylinder. Soon this transfer to sound from record to air was being carried out using an electronic pick-up head, and now of course the whole operation can be completed electronically on a tape recorder. I would like to see electronics produce some form of musical instrument which could take its place in society in the same way that the musical box did in the nineteenth century. Already it is possible to buy a small electronic organ on which simple music can be played. Perhaps a development of this could be a small electronic instrument on which taped music could be played, but which allowed a choice of arrangement and orchestration to the owner.

Some may be surprised at such ideas at the end of a book about antiques. But we must not stand still; we must base new ideas on the resources available. Remember it was this principle that was largely responsible for the invention of the music box in the first place.

APPENDIX A

Directory of the More Important Makers

ABRAHAMS, B. H. Made Britannia disc music boxes and also very many cheap cylinder boxes. Identified by the initials "BHA" and the cases, which were often decorated with a transfer.

ALIBERT, FRANÇOIS Made cylinder boxes in Paris between 1800 and 1850. He made mostly snuffbox movements with sectional combs, but also large movements, a few of which have a one-piece comb. Many of his movements are to be seen in musical clocks. Identified by his name stamped on the bedplate or comb; do not confuse this with his repair work, when the name is scratched on the brass.

AUBERT, A. Made music boxes in Switzerland until 1907, then moved to Clerkenwell where he set up in business with Louis. Jaccard (q.v.). Here they repaired and assembled music boxes. He died in 1910 from consumption.

AUBERT FILS Made musical snuffboxes in Geneva. Identified by the name stamped on the comb.

BAKER, GEORGE, & Co. Made good quality large cylinder boxes often of a complicated nature. The firm was in Geneva in about 1870 and later became Baker-Troll. Identified by the name on the tune sheet.

BALL, BEAVON, & Co. A London firm who acted as agents for Swiss manufacturers. They used their own tune sheets on which the initials "BB & C" were printed.

BAUD, AUGUSTE Records show he was making music boxes in L'Auberson, Switzerland, in 1890.

BAUD FRÈRES This company in L'Auberson are probably the world's leading experts in the repair of antique music boxes. They run an efficient service for repinning cylinders.

BENDER & Co. London agents for Polyphon around 1890.

BENDON, GEORGE, & Co. Made cylinder music boxes in Ste Croix. Their tune sheets are printed with a large coat of arms of the British lion and unicorn, which serves to identify the maker.

BERENS, BLOMBERG, & CIE. Agents for musical box manufacturers in Geneva including François Lecoultre (q.v.). They also had an agency in London. Identified by the initials "BB & C", which makes them hard to distinguish from Ball, Beavon, & Co. (q.v.).

BILLON-HALLER, JEAN Made cylinder boxes in Geneva around 1880.

BONTEMPS, CHARLES Made fine quality singing birds in cages in Paris around 1850. The company has continued until recently.

BORDIER, A. Made fine quality snuffbox movements in Geneva around 1800.

BORDIER, M. Maker of small musical movements of very good quality from 1815–30. Identified by the name stamped on the bedplate or comb.

BORDIER FRÈRES Made high quality small movements from 1815–30. Identified by the name stamped on the bedplate or comb.

BORNAND, ADRIAN Made music boxes in Ste Croix in about 1860.

BORNAND, JOSEPH Nephew of the above. He went to New York in 1883 as a comb tuner for Messrs. Paillard (q.v.).

BORNAND, ADRIAN Son of Joseph, he established the Bornand Music Box Co., Pelham, New York, which is directed today by Mrs Ruth Bornand.

BREITLER, S. A. This company was founded at Ste Croix in 1929, since when it has been mass-producing small movements for toys and souvenirs.

BREMOND, B. A. Made very fine cylinder boxes in Geneva from 1860 onwards. Boxes of all types were made but so far a keywind Bremond machine has not been seen. Identified by the initials "BAB" on the tune sheet or governor bracket and a lyre trade mark on the tune sheet. Often the flat top to the handle of the winding lever is stamped with the serial number.

BRUGGER & STRAUB Makers of cylinder boxes who had an address at

High Holborn, London. Identified by a tune sheet printed with the trade mark of a triangle and striker.

BRUGUIER, CHARLES ABRAM Made fine singing-bird boxes at Geneva in the first half of the nineteenth century in co-operation with his brother Jacques. They also made a very few small cylinder movements, but these are extremely rare. Identified by the name stamped on the movement.

BRUGUIER (the elder) Father of the above, he made fine singing-bird boxes until about 1810.

CADET, DAVID Made cylinder boxes in Geneva around 1820, including what was probably the first four-comb cylinder box, using sectional combs in groups of five teeth.

CAPT, HENRI DANIEL Made good quality musical movements for snuffboxes and watches at Geneva in 1802–11. Many of his movements had sectional movements of unusual design and were often to be found in cases made of tin.

CAPT, HENRI This could be the son of the above, and is known to have been working in Geneva in 1850, making movements for snuffboxes which few other makers could equal. He also made large overture boxes with bells and drum. Identified by the name stamped on the comb.

CONCHON, F. Made good quality boxes in Geneva around 1890. Many of their movements are of unusual type such as Harpe Aeolienne or Sublime Harmony. Cochon also made organ boxes. Identified by the trade mark stamped on the governor bracket. It is a design of two ovals set side by side, the left containing the initials "FCL" and the right a lyre.

CUENDET, ABRAHAM LOUIS Known to have made music boxes in Switzerland in 1810.

CUENDET-DEVELAY FILS & CIE. Makers of music boxes around 1890, they tried to produce an indestructible box of robust design.

CUENDET, JOHN, et Ed. This company was registered at L'Auberson in 1895 but the family were already making good quality music boxes some twenty years before then. They still are most active,

making small movements for toys, souvenirs and other articles.

DAWKINS, THOMAS, & Co. Made good quality boxes in Geneva in 1880–1914. The tone was crisp and the music usually well set. Identified by the trade mark of a sphinx stamped on the governor bracket and printed on the tune sheet. The comb screw washers were often in the form of brass rosettes. There is often a knurled flange at each end of the cylinder.

DUBOIS, CHARLES DANIEL Maker of musical watches at La Chaux de Fonds around 1813.

DUCOMMUN GIROD, F. W. Made music boxes in Geneva in 1840–60. Often the music is embellished with sustained trills, and it is usually well set-up. Also many small movements were made. Identified by the name stamped on the bedplate or comb and the trade mark on the tune sheet of a sunburst containing a face.

DUTERTE, AUGUSTE Musical box maker in Geneva around 1850.

FALCONNET & REYMOND Known to have made very fine overture boxes in Geneva in 1830. Identified by the name stamped on the comb or bedplate.

FAVRE, ANTOINE Made the first musical box to use a tuned tooth comb, in 1796.

FLOTE, GEORGE It has been recorded that he was making musical watches in Islington in 1800.

GAVIOLI, L. Maker of barrel organs in London around 1890, whose company later became one of the major fair-organ manufacturers.

GREINER, T. H. Made music boxes in Geneva, and for some time worked in cooperation with Bremond (q.v.).

GUEISSAZ FILS, & Co. This company was registered at L'Auberson in 1849 when it made good quality music boxes. It still exists there, mass-producing small movements.

HELLER, J. H. Made good quality large music boxes in Bern around 1870. Many of their boxes had organ accompaniment. Identified by the name on the tune sheet.

HENRIOT Made music boxes in Geneva around 1850. Identified by the name stamped on the bedplate.

Imhof & Mukle Predecessor of Imhof's in New Oxford Street, London, they made barrel orchestrions and were agents for other makers of mechanical musical instruments.

Jaccard, Alexis Maker of small movements in Ste Croix around 1870.

Jaccard, Edouard Brother of the above. The two worked together as Jaccard Frères.

Jaccard, Les Fils De John Founded at Ste Croix by Jules Jaccard in 1862, this company still manufactures there.

Jaccard, Jules Recorded to have made music boxes at Ste Croix in 1862.

Jaccard, Louis Worked with Aubert (q.v.) in Clerkenwell and, after the death of Aubert, continued repairs on phonographs until 1934 when he was killed in a fire which destroyed the workshop.

Jaccard, L. G. Wrote a useful paper, *Origin and Development of the Music Box*, in the *Chicago Hobbies Magazine* in 1938.

Jacot, Charles Henry, & Co. Made music boxes in New York where he invented the Jacot Safety Check, which prevented movements from having an accidental run.

Jacques, Louis & Son Known to have made large music boxes in Le Brassus in 1850.

Janvier Fils, Saloman Made musical boxes in Ste Croix around 1830.

Jaquet-Droz, Pierre Worked in Geneva and Paris with his son, Henri Louis. They made the famous automata the Musician, the Writer and the Draughtsman in the late eighteenth century.

J.G.M. & Co. A company which made small album movements in Paris around 1890. It is not known what the initials stand for.

Junod, Alfred Was making music boxes at Ste Croix in about 1887, and constructed the "Duplex" which played two cylinders at the same time.

Kaarer & Co. Made music boxes in Germany around 1880. Identified by the name on the tune sheet.

KAPT See *Capt*.

LADOR S. A. This company was founded at Ste Croix in 1825. It still exists there making small movements.

LANGDORF & FILS Made music boxes in Geneva in 1850–70. The movements were of good quality and many forte-piano and organ boxes were made. Identified by the trade mark of a carillon keyboard on the tune sheet.

LECOULTRE, C. Made music boxes at Ste Croix. His work is rare and can be identified by his name on the tune sheet.

LECOULTRE, DAVID Made music boxes at Le Brassus from 1810–50. Identified by the distinctive tune sheets, on which is written his name; also the combs have teeth with square tips to them and are usually set on a bedplate of steel.

LECOULTRE & CIE. This firm is in Le Sentier, the headquarters for the company's watchmaking industry. Founded in 1833 to provide a diversification from the musical boxes which were being produced by the family in Geneva.

LECOULTRE ET FALCONNET Made fine quality overture boxes in about 1820.

LECOULTRE, FRANÇOIS He set up in business with Henri, his brother, in Geneva in 1815, where they made many boxes of fine quality.

LECOULTRE FRERES Name of the company which made good quality boxes in Geneva after about 1850. Identified by the letters "LB" or $\frac{\text{"LF"}}{\text{G}^{ve}}$ stamped on the comb.

LECOULTRE, HENRI Worked in partnership with François in Geneva around 1815. His name was often stamped on the comb of the many snuffbox movements he made.

LECOULTRE, L. Maker of small musical movements around 1820.

L'EPÉE, AUGUSTE Made music boxes in St Suzanne, Doubs, France, between 1839 and 1914. He made many boxes for Thibouville-Lamy (q.v.). Identified by the name on the tune sheet, but most of his boxes are not marked.

LEPINE, JEAN ANTOINE Made musical watches in Paris about 1800.

LE ROY Maker of musical watches in Paris in the early nineteenth century.

LESCHOT, JEAN FRÉDÉRIC Made singing birds and automata and lived from 1747 to 1824.

LESCHOT, GEORGE AUGUSTE Son of the above, he made great advances in the technique of watchmaking while working for Vacheron & Constantin (q.v.).

LOCHMANN, PAUL Patented the first disc music box with interchangeable tune sheets at Leipzig in 1885, and from this developed the Symphonion which he started to manufacture the same year. He also made a machine called the Lochmann Original, whose discs had a turned-up lip.

MALIGNON, A. Made music boxes in Geneva in about 1835.

MAILLARDET, HENRI A maker of automata who assisted the Jaquet-Droz (q.v.) with their work in 1780. Also made his own singing birds and automata in London in 1784–1815.

MAILLARDET, PÈRE ET FILS Jean David, son of the above, and his son, Julien Auguste, made automata at Fontaines in the first half of the nineteenth century.

MANGER, JOHN, & Co. Made music boxes at Geneva in about 1860 and later formed partnership with Mojon, Montandon to trade as Mojon Manger & Co. (q.v.).

MARCHAND, A. Maker of good quality snuffbox movements.

MARGOT-CUENDET, A. Maker of musical boxes at L'Auberson.

MARGOT, FRANK Founded at L'Auberson in 1945, this firm makes small movements for toys, souvenirs and manivelles.

MARTINET & BENOIT Maker of good quality musical boxes in Geneva in about 1860. Identified by the name stamped on the comb or bedplate.

MATTHEY S. A. Specialists in musical movements, souvenirs and animated advertisements, this company was founded at Vuiteboeuf in 1929.

MELODIES S. A. This company was founded at Ste Croix as Thorens S.A. in 1883. The name was changed recently.

MERMOD, AUGUSTE This firm makes movements of the small modern type and also miniature movements and combs. It was founded at Grandson in 1937.

MERMOD & BORNAND, G. Musical box makers in Ste Croix.

MERMOD FRÈRES Made music boxes at Ste Croix from 1815 to 1889. The firm consisted of the brothers Gustave, Alfred, Louis Phillipe and Leon Marcel and made a great variety of types of musical box. They fitted penny-in-the-slot operation to many of their machines and were also responsible for the Stella and Mira disc machines. Identified by the trade mark of a five-pointed star.

METERT, HENRY Worked as a mechanic for Nicole Frères (q.v.) from the age of eleven and continued with them until 1903. He started in Geneva and later came to London. When Nicole Frères ceased business in 1903 he continued alone until his death in 1933. Identified by his name stamped on the bedplate or by the trade mark of a piano keyboard standing on three lyre-shaped legs.

MEYLAN, PHILIPPE-SAMUEL Worked in Le Brassus and Geneva making automata and complex watches. He was the first to make musical watches with steel teeth and a disc, according to Baillie, and went to Geneva in 1811 to work in company with L. Audemars and Isaac-Daniel Piguet (q.v.) until 1828. Identified by the initials "PM" stamped on the movement.

MOJON, MANGER, & Co. Made large musical boxes including many with interchangeable cylinders. Identified by the initials "MMC" stamped on the governor bracket.

MOULINIE AINÉ Watchmaker in Geneva in 1829, who made a number of high-class overture boxes. Identified by the name stamped on the bedplate.

NATIONAL MUSIC BOX A subsidiary of the Dawkins Company (q.v.) who had their own tune sheets.

NICOLE, FRANÇOIS Worked in Geneva from 1776–1849, where he made a small number of superb overture boxes whose quality and music has seldom been bettered. The cylinders are scribed with horizontal lines as well as register lines and the combs are

stamped "FRANÇs NICOLE". Later boxes by this maker are stamped "F. Nicole" on the comb or bedplate.

NICOLE FRÈRES It has generally been accepted that this company was formed in Geneva in 1839 by a partnership between the two brothers François and Raymond. Recent researches by Mr C. de Vere Green and Mr A. W. J. G. Ord-Hume have shown that it is highly possible that previous theories are incorrect. Consultation of the Geneva archives indicate that Nicole Frères resulted from a partnership established in about 1815 by the brothers Pierre Moise Nicole and David Elie Nicole. They made more boxes of a consistently good quality than any other maker. They had agents in very many countries including Savory Cox & Co. in London. Their own office in London was in Hatton Garden. After the advent of the disc music box they became foremost selling agents for Polyphon. All Nicole Frères movements are stamped with a serial number and because of this can be dated fairly accurately. John E. T. Clark in his book *Musical Boxes* gives a most useful number and date guide, from which the date of any Nicole Frères music box can be determined:

19,000 were made up to	1839
25,000	1843
27,000	1845
29,000	1847
35,000	1860
38,000	1861
40,000	1863
41,000	1870
43,000	1872
44,000	1880
46,000	1882
50,000	1888
52,000	1903

The serial number is stamped on the bedplate and cylinder and is also written on the tune sheet. Boxes are identified by the

ROCHAT, LES FRÈRES Makers of fine singing birds in Geneva in 1810–1825. They made birds in snuffboxes, cages, parasol handles and three gold pistols each with a bird that sang when the trigger was pulled. Identified by the initials "FR" in a diamond.

ROCHAT, H. Made musical snuffboxes in about 1840. Identified by the name stamped on the comb.

ROCHAT, PIERRE Worked with Jaquet-Droz (q.v.) for a time and then made musical boxes. In 1815 he started to make fine singing birds.

ROEPKE, CARL ALBERT Developed a system of plucking a comb by means of star wheels and a moving strip of card. This system was used effectively in longcase clocks, which were made in Berlin in about 1895.

RZEBITSCHEK, FRANTIZEK Made very good quality music boxes in Prague often for clocks. Identified by the name—sometimes spelled "Rebicek"—stamped on the bedplate. His combs had the base teeth on the right.

SALLAZ & OBOUSSIER Made music boxes in Ste Croix in about 1850. Identified by their name on the tune sheet.

SANDOZ, LOUIS A Swiss maker of small music boxes around 1818.

SLAWIK & PREISZIER Made music boxes in Prague. Identified by their name stamped on the bedplate.

STAUFFER Made good musical boxes in Geneva in about 1878.

THIBOUVILLE-LAMY, JEROME & Co. Made musical boxes in Paris from about 1850 onwards. There are many points of design which make their work easy to recognise. The bedplate is usually made of copper-plated gunmetal and is screwed into the case from below instead of through the sides. The winding lever is usually fitted with a wooden handle, and the wooden partition to which the control levers are attached is screwed together so that the screw heads are visible. The return springs on the stop works and the winding ratchet are doubled back instead of being straight. Finally, the tune sheets are quite long and plain having the words *"Fabrique de Genève"* but seldom the maker's name.

THORENS, HERMANN Made small music boxes from 1846 to 1943 at Ste Croix.

TROLL, SAMUEL The Troll of the Baker-Troll combination in Geneva.

ULLMAN, CHARLES Made good boxes at L'Auberson from 1870 to 1890. He used highly coloured tune sheets and his trade mark was a griffon and shield with the initials "Ch.U."

VAUCANSON, JACQUES DE Born at Grenoble in 1709, died in 1782. He was the maker of the famous three automata, the Duck, the Flute Player and the Drummer, which he took to Paris in 1738.

VACHERON & CONSTANTIN Famous maker of watches who also made good quality small musical boxes in Geneva in the first half of the eighteenth century.

WILLEMBACHER & RZEBITSCHEK Made good quality musical boxes, some for clocks, in Prague in the middle of the nineteenth century. Identified by the name stamped on the bedplate, and the bass teeth being on the right of the comb.

ZIMMERMANN, JULES HEINRICH Made the Fortuna disc musical box at Leipzig in about 1900.

ZUMSTEG, HEINRICH Designed a system of gears by which the playing time of music boxes could be greatly increased. He worked in Kulm, Aargua, Germany around 1885.

APPENDIX B

Glossary

Antiphone: A mechanical piano player which could be put onto the keyboard. The musical score was set on a wooden board with metal pegs.

Automaton: A model of a living creature which contains a mechanism to make it move realistically.

Barrel: The wooden pinned cylinder of a barrel organ or barrel piano.

Barrel Organ: A mechanical instrument which plays pipes or reeds from a pinned barrel.

Barrel Piano: A mechanical instrument which plays piano strings from a pinned barrel.

Bedplate: The metal base upon which the musical movement is constructed.

Bellows: The mechanism which supplies air to organ pipes.

Book Music: Music punched out on cardboard and folded so that it can be played on, say, a fair organ.

Bridge: A metal bearing or support which can be screwed down to carry a working part such as the spring barrel or cylinder, etc.

Carillon: A set of bells which can be played mechanically.

Case: The box or cabinet in which the musical movement is contained.

Cement: A mixture of shellac, pitch and brick dust, which is poured into the cylinder to set the pins.

Click: The retaining pawl which bears on a ratchet wheel.

Clock Pins: Tapered pins made of brass or steel for wedging parts in place.

Comb: The piece of sheet steel, cut in the shape of a comb, which is tuned to play the music of a musical box.

Composition: A mixture of powdered horn and carbon black which can be moulded into snuffboxes and other articles.

Control Levers: The levers which project from the end of a music box case by which it can be started, stopped and made to repeat or change the tune.

Cylinder: The brass tube which bears the musical score, set on it with pins.

Cylinder Arbor: The metal spindle upon which the cylinder revolves.

Cylinder Bridges: The brackets at either end of the cylinder in which the ends of the arbor revolve.

Cylinder End Plates: The two plates which close the ends of the cylinder.

Damper: The piece of flat spring steel wire, pinned under the end of the tooth. The damper stops the vibration of the tooth just before it is plucked again.

Disc: The tune sheet of a disc music box or the pinned platform of the earlier radial miniature movements.

Drive Pin: The metal pin screwed into the great wheel which fits into a slot in the cylinder causing it to rotate.

Duplex: Refers to a musical box which plays two combs or sometimes two cylinders at the same time.

Endflap: The hinged flap at the end of a case which covers the control levers in key-wind boxes.

Endless Screw: A helical gear made of steel which serves to act as a governor when fitted with an air brake.

Endstone: A jewel cut with a flat on one side, usually of garnet. It is held in place on top of the governor bracket so that the flat is over the upper bearing of the endless screw. The top of the endless screw bears against it and revolves on it.

Fan: Another name for the air brake fitted to the endless screw. Adjustment to the fan can control the speed of the mechanism.

Fan Movement: An alternative name for the early radial snuffbox movements.

Forte-piano: A type of musical movement which plays alternating loud and soft passages.

French Polish: A solution of shellac in methylated spirit which can be applied to wood to give a high polish.

Fusee: A spirally grooved pulley of varying diameter interposed between the barrel and the drive pinion of a movement for the purpose of converting the varying force of the mainspring into a constant pressure on the movement.

Gear Train: A sequence of wheels and pinions which gives the connection between the spring and the endless screw.

Geneva Stop: A stop work on the spring barrel which prevents the spring from being over-wound and also stops it from winding right down.

Governor: The mechanism which controls the running speed of a clockwork motor. In the case of musical boxes it is the endless screw.

Governor Bracket: The bracket or cock which carries the jewel on which the top of the endless screw bears.

Great Wheel: The wheel at the governor end of the cylinder arbor.

Instant Stop: The control lever which allows you to stop the movement at will before the tune ends. It should never be used except during adjustment.

Laminated Comb: A comb which is built up in horizontal layers of metal, each layer forming a tooth. Used on very early boxes and in seals.

Leads: Term used sometimes for the resonators.

Mainspring: The steel spring which provides the motive power for the movement.

Movement: The mechanism of a musical box.

Piano-player: A development of the antiphone which uses a paper roll punched with the musical score.

Pinion: Usually made of steel, it is the small gear which meshes with the larger brass wheel.

Pins: The projections in the cylinder which pluck the comb.

Pipe Organ: An organ which plays its music on pipes as opposed to reeds.

Platform Movement: Another name for the early radial snuffbox movement.

Pneumatic Action: This is when the transfer of movement is carried out by air pressure in pipes and not by levers. Fairground organs and pianolas have pneumatic action.

Pressure Bar: The bar which holds a disc down onto the star wheels of a disc music box.

Projections: The points stamped out of a disc which turn the star wheels.

Ratchet: A wheel with pointed teeth which is fixed to a spindle to prevent it turning back. It is held in position by the click.

Reed Organ: An organ which plays on reeds as opposed to pipes.

Register: The alignment of the comb to the cylinder so that its teeth select the correct time.

Resonator: The piece of lead attached to the underside of a comb tooth, which causes it to vibrate at the desired speed. Treble teeth vibrate so quickly that a resonator is not necessary.

Run: A run occurs when part of the wheel train of a musical movement breaks. The cylinder then revolves suddenly until the spring is unwound. This causes great damage to the movement.

Safety Check: A device invented by Mermod which puts a brake on the great wheel as soon as the cylinder begins to run.

Snail: The spiral ramp on which the cylinder rests and which causes the tune to change by moving the cylinder sideways into different positions against the comb.

Stop Arm: The control lever, which allows the movement to stop at the end of a tune.

Stop Tail: A small metal arm pushed on to the endless screw which is caught by the stop work when the movement stops at the end of a tune.

Stop Work: The mechanism on the side of the wheel train which slips into a notch in the great wheel and also checks the stop bar on the endless screw.

Star Wheel: Star-shaped wheels which are set over the comb of a disc

machine and cause the comb to play when they are turned by the action of the disc revolving over them.

Sublime Harmony: An arrangement of combs where two or more combs are tuned to almost the same pitch. A slight difference in pitch causes "beats" which give the tone of the box great resonance.

Teeth: The tuned metal "notes" of a comb, or sometimes the teeth of a gear wheel.

Tips: The tapered points of the teeth which are shaped so that they can be plucked by the cylinder pins.

Tune Changer: A bar attached to the bedplate with a finger which impinges on the snail and rotates it to change the tune.

Tune Indicator: A quadrant dial with a pointer which bears on the end of the cylinder and indicates on the dial the number of the tune being played.

Tune Selector: A manually operated lever attached to the bedplate which can turn the snail to change the tune at will.

Tune Sheet: The card on the lid of the music box on which the tunes to be played are written. Also the metal discs of disc machines are sometimes called tune sheets.

Two-per-Turn: A type of musical box with a large diameter cylinder, which plays two tunes for every revolution of the cylinder.

Wheel: A gear, often of brass, which meshes with a pinion, usually made of steel.

Wheel Train: See *Gear Train.*

Wind Chest: The air reservoir in a pneumatic machine. It is pumped up with the bellows and the air is let into the instrument as required. Pressure is usually maintained by means of a spring.

Zither: This instrument of Tyrol origin is a wooden box over which strings are stretched. It is plucked and its tone can be imitated on a music box by the "zither attachment", a roll of tissue paper which touches the comb as it plays.

APPENDIX C

Bibliography

ARCHER, M.: *Tippoo's Tiger* (Victoria and Albert Museum, London, 1959).

BAILLIE, G. H.: *Watchmakers and Clockmakers of the World* (N.A.G. Press, London, 1963).

BOSTON, the late Canon, and LANGWILL, Lyndesay G.: *Church and Chamber Barrel Organs* (Boston & Langwill, Edinburgh, 1967).

BOWERS, Q. David: *Guidebook of Automatic Musical Instruments* (Vestal Press, New York, 1968). Two volumes.

BOWERS, Q. David: *Put Another Nickel In* (Vestal Press, New York, 1966).

BRADBURY, F.: *British and Irish Silver Assay Office Marks* 1544–1963 (J. W. Northend Ltd., Sheffield, 1964).

BUCHNER, Dr Alexander: *Mechanical Musical Instruments* (Batchworth Press, Spring House, London, 1954). Now scarce.

CHAPUIS, Alfred: *Histoire de la Boite à Musique* (Edition Scripta, Lausanne, 1955). Now scarce.

CHAPUIS, Alfred, and DROZ, Edmond: *Automata* (Editions du Griffon, Neuchatel, 1958: English translation, B. T. Batsford Ltd., London).

CHAPUIS, Alfred, and GELIS, Edward: *Le Monde des Automates* (Societie Anonyme, Paris, 1928). Now very rare.

CLARKE, John E. T.: *Musical Boxes* (George Allen and Unwin Ltd., London, 1961).

COCKAYNE, Eric V.: *How the Fair Organ Works* (Fair Organ Preservation Society, Northampton, 1968).

FRIED, Frederick: *A Pictorial History of the Carousel* (A. S. Barnes, New York and London, 1964).

GIVENS, Larry: *Rebuilding the Player Piano* (Vestal Press, New York, 1963).

JACCARD, L. G.: *The Origin and Development of Music Boxes* (Chicago Hobbies Magazine, 1938).

JACOT, C. H.: *How to Repair Musical Boxes* (New York 1890:, facsimile reprint by Musical Box Society of Great Britain Journal, 1967, Vol. 3, No. 2).

MAINGOT, Éliane: *Les Automates* (Librairie Hachette, Paris, 1959).

MOSORIAK, Roy: *The Curious History of Music Boxes* (Lightner Publishing Co., Chicago, 1943). Now scarce.

ORD-HUME, Arthur: *Collecting Musical Boxes and How to Repair Them* (George Allen and Unwin, London, 1967, and Crown, New York).

ORD-HUME, Arthur: *Player Piano—The History of the Mechanical Piano and How to Repair it* (George Allen and Unwin, London, 1970 and A. S. Barnes, New York, 1969).

PRASTEAU, Jean: *Les Automates* (Librairie Grund, Paris, 1968).

ROEHL, Harvey: *The Player Piano Treasury* (Vestal Press, New York, 1964).

SCHOLES, Percy A.: *The Oxford Companion to Music* (Oxford University Press, 1942).

TARDY: *Les Poinçons de Garantie pour l'Or* (Joseph Floch, Paris, 1966).

TARDY: *Les Poinçons de Garantie pour l'Argent* (Joseph Floch, Paris, 1966).

WAARDE, R. de: *From Music Boxes to Street Organs* (Vestal Press, New York, 1967).

WEBB, Graham: *The Cylinder Musical Box Handbook* (Faber & Faber, London, 1968, and Fernhill House, New York, 1969).

WEBB, Graham: *The Disc Musical Box Handbook* (Faber & Faber, London, 1970).

The Music Box—Journal of the Musical Box Society of Great Britain (London, 1962 onwards).

Bulletin of the Musical Box Society International (U.S.A., 1965 onwards).

INDEX

Abrahams, B. H., 58
accordion, mechanical, 81
acrobat automaton, 92
Aeolian Orchestrelle, 80
Alibert, François, 27
Ariston organette, 83
Auber: *Crown Diamonds*, 42;
    Fra Diavolo, 37
Aubert, Moise, 14
automata, 84–96: in clocks, 87;
    origins of, 87
automaton: acrobat, 92; musical box,
   72; draughtsman, 89; magician, 92;
   monkey, 91; musician, 88; picture,
   93–4; smoker, 92; watch, 73;
   writer, 89

barking dog watch, 73
barrel orchestrion, 77
barrel organ, 11, 13, 23, 74
Baud Frères, 106, 116
bedplate, 15, 24, 28, 100-1, 109
Bellini: *Norma*, 37; *La Sonnambula*, 37
bells, 11-13, 48, 57-9, 72: manivelles
   with, 28
birdboxes; see Singing Birdboxes
bird organ, 75
birdsong, imitation of, 64–9, 90
Bishop, Henry Rowley: *Bid me
   discourse*, 42; *Home Sweet Home*,
   42; Thalberg variations on *Home
   Sweet Home*, 42
Bontemps: Charles, 86, 90, 116;
   Lucienne, 92; Seraphim, 86
book music, 88
Boom, Miguel, 52

Bordier, M., 26
Bornand, Ruth, 50
Bowes Museum, 95
Brackhausen, Gustave, 53-6
Breguet, 13
Bremond, B. A., 41
Britannia disc machine, 58
Bruguier, Charles Abraham, 68
buying: birdbox, 70; cylinder box,
   97-112; disc box, 62, 111; musical
   seal, 70; musical watch, 72

cabin trunk snuffbox, 22
Capital Cuff Box, 59
Capt, Henri, 14, 26-7, 71
carillon, 11-13, 23, 72, 74
Caruso, 17
case, 15, 38-40, 55, 58, 61, 91;
   decoration, 39; inner glass lid to,
   43; repairs to, 102
castanet, 50
Chaillet, Octave, 54-5
change lever, 16, 39
Chapuis, Alfred, 64
Chapuis & Droz, 85, 93
Clark, John, 31
clock: musical, 27, 31, 61; with
   striking jacks, 87; Polyphon clock,
   61
clockwork: invention of, 11, 87;
   repairs to, 63
cock, 15, 24
comb: adjustment, 108; laminated, 13,
   24, 70; one-piece, 13, 24, 33;
   removal of, 100; sectional, 13, 14,
   24, 28; tuning, 44, 54, 103-4

139

MUSIC BOXES:
A Guide for Collectors